Accelerate

● ● ● ● ● ● ● ● ● ●

A SKILLS-BASED
SHORT COURSE

BEGINNER

Series editor: Philip Prowse

SARAH SCOTT-MALDEN · JUDITH WILSON

Heinemann English Language Teaching
Halley Court, Jordan Hill, Oxford OX2 8EJ
A division of Reed Educational & Professional Publishing Limited

OXFORD MADRID FLORENCE ATHENS PRAGUE
SÃO PAULO MEXICO CITY CHICAGO PORTSMOUTH (NH)
TOKYO SINGAPORE KUALA LUMPUR MELBOURNE
AUCKLAND JOHANNESBURG IBADAN GABORONE

Heinnemann is a registered trademark of
Reed Educational & Professional Publishing Limited

ISBN 0 435 28257 3

Designed by Portfolio Design Consultancy, Aylesbury
Cover design by Threefold Design
Cover photograph by Frank Orel/Tony Stone Images

The publishers would like to thank *Young Telegraph* for
'Blinding Success'.

Printed in East Kilbride, Scotland by Thomson Litho Ltd

97 98 99 10 9 8 7 6 5 4 3

Contents

Map of the book

Unit 1

Me Myself I

Lesson 1 Me... 2
Lesson 2 Things in common 4
Lesson 3 On my own 6

Unit 2

Just a dream

Lesson 1 Dream hotel 8
Lesson 2 Dream car 10
Lesson 3 Dream day 12

Unit 3

Free time

Lesson 1 I like music 14
Lesson 2 Sports crazy 16
Lesson 3 Almost real 18

Unit 4

Talking

Lesson 1 Nice to meet you! 20
Lesson 2 Get in touch 22
Lesson 3 Can you talk about it? 24

Unit 5

The first time

Lesson 1 Can you remember? 26
Lesson 2 First job 28
Lesson 3 Are you old enough? 30

Unit 6

Let's be friends

Lesson 1 Just good friends 32
Lesson 2 How did you meet? 34
Lesson 3 Living alone, living together 36

Unit 7

Away from home

Lesson 1 Leaving home 38
Lesson 2 In another country 40
Lesson 3 Let the kids pay the bills 42

Unit 8

It's my world

Lesson 1 Before I'm old 44
Lesson 2 See the world 46
Lesson 3 Time for a change 48

Unit 9

Learning for life

Lesson 1 Exam time 50
Lesson 2 Changing places 52
Lesson 3 Something new 54

Unit 10

Let's celebrate

Lesson 1 What a lovely present! 56
Lesson 2 Party time 58
Lesson 3 It's the end 60

Test 62

Tapescripts 66

Views of language learning

Create two images in your mind: a large oak tree growing in a green field, and a large jigsaw puzzle of a tree which is partly completed.

What has this got to do with language learning? Simply the images of oak and jigsaw represent differing ways of looking at language learning. For many people, learning a language is like doing a jigsaw: the language is broken up into lots of little bits and they are pieced together, one by one, until the whole picture is built up. Incredibly, despite all the discussion over language learning in the last quarter of a century, this is still a popular view and lessons are expected to contain one grammatical point at a time. The bit of grammar is learnt just like that, and the learner goes on to the next bit. Regrettably therefore, most learners leave their English classes with only part of the picture – rather like the partly-done jigsaw you imagined. Leonard Newmark expressed this well nearly thirty years ago in 'How not to interfere with language learning' (*International Journal of American Linguistics*, 32, January 1966):

'If the task of learning to speak English were additive and linear [...] the child learner would be old before he [*sic*] could say a single appropriate thing and the adult learner would be dead.'

The other view compares language learning to the oak. It is natural, growing and changing. An oak is still an oak whether it is the mighty tree you may have imagined or a tiny sapling. All trees are unique, yet share similar characteristics. In this view of language learning, learners learn by doing, by using the language in contexts that interest them. Different learners will learn different things from the same lesson – in the language classroom there is no one-to-one correspondence between learning and teaching, or as David Nunan put it at IATEFL in 1994, 'Why Don't Learners Learn What Teachers Teach?'. The differences between the two approaches are summarized by Dave Willis in *The Lexical Syllabus* (Collins, 1990):

'Form-focused approaches see language as a system of patterns or structures [...] Task-based approaches see language as a system of meanings.'

What's in *Accelerate*?

The oak and jigsaw also help us with the problem of what to include in a book or course. When a jigsaw is complete nothing can be added to it. An oak is never complete – it grows and changes throughout its life. The fallacy of completeness encourages learners to believe that if they ingest the textbook lesson-by-lesson, they will have swallowed the whole of the English language. Nothing could be further from the truth. Any course, any book, can only offer a sample of English. We can expect this sample to be interesting, and generative, in that it will encourage further language learning, but we cannot expect it to be a piece of the jigsaw, which, when fitted together, gives the whole language picture. The four levels of *Accelerate* are not intended to be done one after the other: they are suited to short course students at four different levels. They enable students to grow and develop at their own pace, acknowledging that learning English is something that continues and is not confined to the classroom.

We favour learning by doing. The approach in *Accelerate* is skills based, starting with language use about motivating topics. While each lesson focuses on language form appropriate to the level, that language form is there because the learners need it to carry out the activities and process the texts. Texts and activities are not devised in order to contextualize a pre-specified language syllabus. The language syllabus comes from the texts and activities themselves.

Using *Accelerate*

In creating these materials our aim has been to produce lessons that work: lessons that are transparent to the teacher and student. Each lesson takes a double-page spread, with a clear language focus and skills-summary box. Practice pages for each lesson give vital reinforcement of language focus points and help those learners who like to do extra work on their own. Flexibility is the keynote of *Accelerate*. The Student's Book provides the core, with its combination of lessons and practice pages; the Teacher's Book contains extra ideas for warmers and extension activities, enabling each teacher to tailor the materials to his or her class needs. The clarity and simplicity of the materials cuts teacher preparation time to a minimum and enables the teacher to concentrate on what he or she is best at – relating to and interacting with the students.

For some groups and teachers it will be appropriate to work through the lesson material step-by-step, and then look at the practice pages in class. For others, particularly mixed ability groups, the teacher may wish to refer to the Practice pages before, or during, an activity to clarify a language point. Where time is very short, Practice pages can be done out of class and the suggested homework omitted. Where there is more time, doing the Practice pages in class gives the teacher an opportunity to pay attention to individuals and do some remedial work. Most of the homework activities can also become classwork, if necessary, and we find that starting or ending a lesson by returning homework from a previous lesson is a valuable way of reviewing, particularly when students are able to read, compare and discuss each other's work. The homework is usually suitable for classroom display and will very quickly give an identity to the group and the room.

Most importantly *Accelerate* focuses on the learner: on his or her interests, experience, and ambitions. The great strength of starting from language skills rather than form is that the materials address the learner as a mature human-being. The learner is seen as someone with a lot to offer who may not speak a lot of English, rather than as someone to be addressed as if they were a child because they do not know much English. The word *accelerate* carries with it the idea of speed. These materials do not offer the possibility of covering the same familiar ground in some magically faster way. However they do enable learners to go faster by extending and revising their command of the language through activities that involve them as people.

Accelerate does not cover the whole of English grammar or the whole of the English language. What it does offer are a number of exciting windows into English, and opportunities for learners to climb through those windows and make English their own.

Map of the book

	Language focus	Skills focus
Unit 1 *Me Myself I*		
Lesson 1 Me... Giving personal information	Present simple *Yes/No* questions	**Listening** for main idea and detail **Speaking:** giving personal information
Lesson 2 Things in common Comparing personal information	Present simple Adjectives to describe appearance	**Reading** and **listening** for detail
Lesson 3 On my own How independent are you?	Adverbs of frequency *a/an* with jobs	**Speaking:** expressing opinions **Reading** a quiz
Unit 2 *Just a dream*		
Lesson 1 Dream hotel Hotel amenities	*can* for possibility	**Reading** for specific information **Writing** holiday postcards
Lesson 2 Dream car Describing cars	Adjectives with and without nouns Prepositions	**Writing** a description
Lesson 3 Dream day Talking about a perfect day	*want to* + verb Prepositions	**Listening** for main idea **Writing** a weekend plan
Unit 3 *Free time*		
Lesson 1 I like music Giving opinions about different types of music	Expressing likes and dislikes Question forms with *What* and *How*	**Listening** for main idea and detail **Speaking:** expressing feelings
Lesson 2 Sports crazy An unusual football fan	*like* + *ing* and *like* + noun	**Reading** a newspaper article for main idea and detail **Listening** for main idea and detail
Lesson 3 Almost real A computer game experience	Present continuous Location and direction	**Listening** for detail **Speaking:** describing events
Unit 4 *Talking*		
Lesson 1 Nice to meet you! How to get talking	Question tags *can* for requests	**Listening** for main idea and detail **Speaking:** starting and continuing a conversation
Lesson 2 Get in touch Advertisements and phone messages	Present continuous for future plans Clauses of purpose	**Listening** for main idea and detail **Writing** an advertisement and replying to an advertisement
Lesson 3 Can you talk about it? Who we talk to	Revision of question words Possessive adjectives Prepositions after verbs – *to, about*	**Listening** for main idea and detail **Speaking:** interviewing people
Unit 5 *The first time*		
Lesson 1 Can you remember? Remembering the past	Past simple Time references	**Reading** for main idea **Speaking:** talking about past events
Lesson 2 First job Comparing school and work	Comparatives Past simple negative	**Reading** for main idea and detail **Speaking:** a roleplay about jobs
Lesson 3 Are you old enough? The best age to be...	Superlatives *should* for expressing opinion	**Reading** for detail **Listening** to complete a text

	Language focus	Skills focus

Unit 6 *Let's be friends*

Lesson 1 Just good friends What makes a good friend	Joining sentences with *and* and *but* *it* as subject with adjectives	**Speaking:** exchanging opinions **Writing** a short poem
Lesson 2 How did you meet? How friends first met	Imperatives Sequencers	**Reading** for main ideas **Writing** a story
Lesson 3 Living alone, living together Sharing accommodation	Expressing similarities and differences *could* for possibility	**Listening** for detail **Speaking:** taking part in a discussion

Unit 7 *Away from home*

Lesson 1 Leaving home Living away from home	Revision of present simple and past simple Expressions of time	**Reading** for detail **Writing** notes and messages
Lesson 2 In another country Living in a different country	*can* and *could* for ability	**Listening** for main idea **Writing:** giving information about your region
Lesson 3 Let the kids pay the bills An unusual family move	Subject and object pronouns Possessive adjectives *must* for necessity	**Reading** for detail **Speaking:** roleplaying a phone conversation

Unit 8 *It's my world*

Lesson 1 Before I'm old Hopes and fears for the future	Future with *will* and *might* for prediction Giving reasons using *because*	**Listening** for main ideas **Speaking:** making decisions and giving reasons
Lesson 2 See the world Travelling and working abroad	Relative clauses with *where* Time sequencers	**Reading** longer texts **Speaking:** roleplaying a radio interview
Lesson 3 Time for a change Changing lifestyles	Future with *going to* *somewhere, something, someone*	**Listening** for detail **Writing** about future plans

Unit 9 *Learning for life*

Lesson 1 Exam time Exam stories	Past continuous and past simple	**Reading** instructions **Listening** for main idea and detail
Lesson 2 Changing places A father goes back to school	*have to* and *had to* for obligation *make, do* and *have*	**Reading** a newspaper article for specific information
Lesson 3 Something new Learning new skills out of school	*-ing* form or infinitive?	**Speaking:** roleplaying a conversation **Listening** for main ideas **Writing** a formal letter

Unit 10 *Let's celebrate*

Lesson 1 What a lovely present! Giving and receiving presents	Expressions for special occasions Relative clauses with *who*	**Listening** for detail **Writing** a letter of thanks
Lesson 2 Party time Having a party	Ways of describing people Invitations	**Listening** for detail and main idea **Speaking:** roleplaying a phone conversation
Lesson 3 It's the end Celebrating the year 2000	Revision of verb forms Talking about dates and times	**Reading** for main idea and detail **Speaking:** planning a celebration

This opening unit focuses on the students themselves, their lives, possessions and personal characteristics.

Lesson 1 *Me*

Aim: To introduce students to some of the language they need to give basic facts about themselves.

Language focus

1 Present simple of **have got**, **be** and other verbs with **I, you, he** and **she**
I**'ve got** a motorbike but I haven't got a car.
He**'s** 22.
He **lives** in London.

2 *Yes/no* **questions**
Have you got a car?
Do you like sport?

Skills focus

- **Listening:** to an interview for main idea and detail
- **Speaking:** giving personal information

Vocabulary focus

- Everyday verbs: *have got, be, live, like*
- Possessions: *car, motorbike, television, guitar, computer*
- Pets: *cat, dog*
- Sport: *football, skiing*

Note

Before beginning this first lesson it is important to know something about the language background and level of the class. This lesson is suitable for a class of mixed beginners/elementary students or false beginners, but a class of complete beginners will need more help and possibly some translation, particularly as the students may be having to cope with new activities as well as the new language.

Warmer

Begin the lesson by introducing yourself and teaching the students how to say their names (*I'm.../My name's...*). With a multilingual class, also teach the pattern *I'm from...* and use a map if available.

Note Throughout the book there is an emphasis on the use of short forms so that the students get used to hearing and using them and can establish the normal patterns of English stress.

1

Ask the students to work in pairs and try to match the words in Activity 1 to the pictures. Find out how many of the words the class recognize. Teach the remaining words and practise pronunciation and word stress.

Answers

a car	*d*
a computer	*a*
a dog	*g*
a guitar	*e*
a motorbike	*c*
a television	*f*

2

🔊 Introduce Pete. Go through the instructions for Activity 2 carefully. Do the first one as an example. Then play the rest of the first part of the cassette and repeat if necessary.

Answers

The students should tick *motorbike, guitar, computer, cat, dog.*

🔊 Now play the second part of the cassette. Then ask students if they can remember what Pete says about the motorbike. (*I've got a motorbike.*) Continue to elicit the other sentences with *I've got ... a guitar/a computer/a cat/a dog.* Play the cassette again and elicit the negative form. (*I haven't got a car/a television.*)

3

Give one or two true sentences about yourself using the same language. (*I've got a television. I haven't got a motorbike.*) Next elicit a few true sentences from different students in the class. Then put the students into pairs and continue with Activity 3. Monitor to check the form of *I've got/I haven't got* and the students' pronunciation.

4

🔊 Although the students are not able to produce these questions at this stage, they may be able to recognize some of them. Ask them to try the activity, working in pairs if they want to. Do not give feedback immediately, but when the students have had sufficient time, play the cassette so that they can check their answers.

Answers

2 *d*	**3** *a*	**4** *b*	**5** *f*	**6** *e*

Practise these questions and answers with the class as a whole. Then they practise in pairs, making a dialogue.

At this stage you could refer to Practice page 66 Language Summary 1. The students have already met and used most of the examples of first person verbs (*I've got/haven't got; I'm/I'm not; I live/I don't live*). Build from the first person to the second and third persons, using the examples in Language Summary 1.

5

This activity moves from the first person (*I*) to the third person (*he*) but the verb forms are given so the students do not have to produce them yet. The focus is still on the content – Pete himself – rather than on the grammatical forms.

Answers

2 *London*
3 *student*
4 *car*
5 *motorbike*
6 *football*
7 *dog*
8 *cat*
9 *computer*
10 *guitar*
11 *television*

6

As an introduction to this activity, you could do a diagram about yourself on the board, similar to the one in Activity 5. The focus now moves to the students themselves. They complete a similar diagram about themselves. Keep the drawings very simple so that there is an element of guesswork. At this stage they may ask for new vocabulary relating to their lives, eg jobs, interests and possessions. You might like to do a diagram about yourself on the board now.

7

Demonstrate this activity by asking one student about his or her diagram. You could also use your diagram and invite students to ask you questions about it.
As feedback, invite some students to give information about their partner. At this stage, introduce *she* for third person female subjects.

Homework

This is very controlled written consolidation of the feedback from Activity 6.

Practice *page 66*

Language Summary 1

Refer back to Lesson 1 Activity 2.
Elicit what Pete said about the motorbike and car. (*I've got a motorbike but I haven't got a car.*) Use this example as a basis and elicit the forms used with *you* and *he/she*.
Then ask the students how old Pete is to elicit *He's 22* and teach *You're/He's/She's* with appropriate ages. Expand this to include the negative forms.
Finally, ask students where Pete lives and deal with *I/you/he/she* forms of other verbs.
Depending on the level of your class, either continue to discuss full forms of these verbs or leave this until a later lesson.

1

In this activity the students are producing sentences with the affirmative and negative forms of the verbs from the lesson. Practise orally – there is one word for each space – and then ask students to write the answers.

Answers

2 I've got a TV but *I haven't got* a computer.
3 He likes dogs but *he doesn't like* cats.
4 He isn't a student, *he's* a teacher.
5 Carmen doesn't live in Madrid, *she lives* in Barcelona.

2

Copy one or two statements from Exercise 2 onto the board and demonstrate the activity and the concept of *true/false* by doing it for yourself, either orally or in writing. Then ask the students to write their own answers and correct statements.

Language Summary 2

Refer back to Lesson 1 Activity 4.
Focus on the *yes/no* **questions** the interviewer asks Pete (5 and 6). Discuss the formation of *yes/no* **questions** using Language Summary 2. (**Wh- questions** may also be learnt as formulae at this stage.)

3

This exercise practises the question forms, focusing on word order, and also introduces students to short answers. Again, they are giving personal responses to the questions.

Answers

2 *Have you got a cat?*
3 *Do you like television?*
4 *Do you live in London?*
5 *Are you 22 years old?*
6 *Does your friend like sport?*
7 *Has your friend got a car?*

Lesson 2 *Things in common*

Aims: To focus on similarities and differences between people and to introduce plural forms of the present simple.

Language focus

1 Present simple with *we* and *they*
We**'re** both quite tall.
We**'ve** both got glasses.
They both **like** sport.

2 Adjectives to describe appearance
He's got **short fair** hair.
She's got **dark** eyes.

Skills focus

- **Listening:** to personal descriptions for detail
- **Reading:** a short magazine article to check facts

Vocabulary focus

- Adjectives: *tall, short, long, fair, dark*
- Personal features: *hair, eyes, glasses*
- Colours: *blue, black, green*
- Clothes: *jeans, T shirt*
- Interests: *sport, watching TV, reading magazines*

Review

Ask students to check the sentences their partners wrote about them for homework. If possible, take photos of the students and make a profile display on the wall. This will provide a link with the idea of the magazine 'Profile' mentioned in this lesson.

1

This reviews the language of the last unit and also introduces the concept of comparing two people. Once students have found two people who reply *yes* to any of the questions, they could extend the activity to ask about other things, eg cars, guitars, televisions, computers, or other vocabulary they learnt in the first lesson.

2

Use the photograph to introduce the language of personal description. Then when the students have answered the questions about Mike and Emma, extend the same language to people in the class, eg *Who's got long hair in this class? Who's got dark eyes?* etc.

Answers

2 *Mike*   3 *Emma*
4 *Mike*   5 *Mike and Emma*   6 *Emma*

3

The students now have to guess or predict the answers to further questions about Mike. Make sure that they understand that they are guessing from the photo but don't have enough information to be sure at this stage.

Play the cassette so that students can compare their guesses with the true information.

Answers

2 *quite tall*   3 *blue*
4 *blue clothes/jeans*   5 *sport*

4

Next, the students listen to Mike comparing himself and Emma. The students have to find the true statements in the list. Give them time to read through the sentences and deal with any vocabulary problems before they listen. Play the cassette once. Ask students to compare answers with a partner. Then play the cassette again.

Answers

| 2 *true* | 3 *false* | 4 *false* | 5 *false* | 6 *false* |
| 7 *false* | 8 *true* | 9 *false* | 10 *true* | 11 *true* |

5

Check the students understand the meaning of *both* by referring back to Activity 1. Then demonstrate the activity by finding something you have in common with a student, eg *you both wear glasses/live in the same town*, etc. After that ask students to do the activity, working first in pairs and then in fours.

You could end up by seeing if there is anything the whole class has in common.

6

This reading text recycles information about Emma from the listening passages and uses vocabulary and structures from Lessons 1 and 2. It contains eight mistakes (of content not language).

Look at the corrected example with the class. Then ask students to try this activity individually. Finally they compare answers in pairs. If students are having difficulty remembering the information, play the cassette from Activity 4 again or give them a copy of the tapescript and refer them to the photo of Emma.

Answers

2 lives in *Oxford* (not London)
3 she's quite *tall* (not short)
4 she's got long *dark hair* (not fair)
5 and *dark eyes* (not blue)
6 she likes *black clothes* (not blue)
7 she *doesn't* like sport
8 she *likes* watching TV

7

The reading text in Activity 6 provides a model for the profiles of members of the class which students write for homework. In order to do this, they need to gather information about one another. They can use the questions in Activity 7 or attempt to make questions of their own. Do not expect complete accuracy during this stage but aim for accuracy for the homework activity.

Homework

Advise students to write six sentences on the same pattern as the profile of Emma.

Practice *page 67*

Language Summary 1

Refer students back to Lesson 2 Activity 4.
Ask who *they* refers to (Mike and Emma). Ask students to find one example of *they* + the verb *to be*, one example of *they* + *have got* and one example of *they* with a regular verb. Then elicit what pronoun Mike uses in the listening passage to refer to himself and Emma (*we*). Establish the forms used with *we*, using Language Summary 1.

1

The mistakes in Exercise 1 are grammatical mistakes and all involve verb concord.

Answers

2 correct
3 He *hasn't* got...
4 correct
5 They *are...*
6 correct
7 He often *wears...*
8 correct
9 correct
10 We *wear...*

2

In this exercise students have to choose the correct verb and the correct form.

Answers

2 *is*
3 *has got*
4 *is*
5 *are*
6 *have got*
7 *has got*

Language Summary 2

Ask students to remember as many adjectives as they can from the lesson. Establish the two key points about adjective use in English, given in Language Summary 2.
You could also ask students to try to work out a rule for adjective order in descriptions, when two adjectives precede a noun. (The colour adjective goes immediately before the noun, eg *short fair* hair, *big blue* eyes.)

3

In Exercise 3 students write true information about themselves and their teacher.

4

This text is a profile of Mike, using the same pattern as the one about Emma. Students can look back to the lesson to find the information if they can't remember it.

Answers

2 *is*	3 *lives*	4 *blue*	5 *short*
6 *blue*	7 *likes*	8 *likes*	

5

Introduce students to a vocabulary network on the topic of personal description. In addition to the words given, encourage students to add any other words they have learnt on the same topic.
You may want to make vocabulary networks regularly during the course as the students meet new topics.

Answers

1 *fair*
2 *jeans*
3 *blue*
4 *short*
(Other words that could be added: *green/black/T-shirt*)

Lesson 3 *On my own*

Aims: For the students to learn the language to describe personal characteristics and to relate these to particular jobs.

Language focus

1 Adverbs of frequency (with present simple)
I **often** go shopping on my own.
I **don't often** go to cafes on my own.
I **never** go to discos on my own.

2 *a/an* with jobs
She's **a** doctor.
He's **an** engineer.

Skills focus

- **Speaking:** expressing opinions about personal qualities and jobs
- **Reading:** a quiz

Vocabulary focus

- **Jobs:** *art teacher, bank manager, doctor, engineer*
- **Personal qualities:** *artistic, clever, friendly, good with numbers/people, independent, kind, practical*
- **Common activities:** *go to cafés/discos, go to school/work/the doctor, go shopping, do your homework*

Review

Add the profiles from Lesson 2 to the wall display about the class begun in Lesson 1, or start a class magazine.

Warmer

Elicit any jobs that the students already know.

1

Ask students to match the jobs to the pictures. Then practise sentences with the pattern *he/she's a/an...* .
Ask the students to suggest when we use *a* and when we use *an*.

Answers

   2 *art teacher*   **3** *doctor*   **4** *bank manager*

2

Before beginning Activity 2, either pre-teach the new vocabulary or use this opportunity to practise dictionary skills. Students give their own opinions in the sentences, which they will then have a chance to compare with a cassette. There are no fixed answers to this activity.

3

Play the cassette of a student doing the activity the students have just completed. Ask the students to write down the qualities suggested and compare them with their own ideas.

Answers

art teacher:	*artistic, good with people, practical*
doctor:	*clever, good with people, kind*
bank manager:	*good with numbers, good with people, independent*

4

In this activity, students choose a partner but at first they work individually. They note down what qualities they think they have, and the job they would be good at. They then do the same for their partner, still without talking to him/her. Finally they compare with their partner and find out their partner's view of them.

5

This quiz focuses on one particular quality - independence. Each student should work individually. Circulate and help as necessary. When the students have finished, explain the marking scheme. Then ask them to add up their marks and read the comments next to their score.
The students may like to compare their results with friends. It is probably best not to conduct a class feedback as some students may not want everyone to know their result.
If your class are able, they may like to discuss whether it is a good thing or not to be very independent.

Homework

This is a written consolidation of the language in Unit 1. It gives the students an opportunity to tell their teacher about themselves using all the aspects covered in Unit 1: personal details, possessions, appearance, likes and dislikes and personal qualities.

Practice *page 68*

Language Summary 1

Refer back to Lesson 3 Activity 5.
Ask the students to make a sentence about something they often do. Point out the position of **often** in the sentence (before the verb). Repeat this procedure with **not often** and **never**.
Contrast this with the position of the adverbs of frequency with the verb **to be**, using Language Summary 1.
Teach the other three common adverbs of frequency, **sometimes**, **usually** and **always**, and point out that these are used in the same way. You could ask students to add *usually* to the diagram (between *often* and *always*).

1

Exercise 1 focuses on the position of the adverb.

Answers

2 *They always go shopping on Saturdays.*
3 *We don't often watch television.*
4 *I usually do my homework before dinner.*
5 *He never wears glasses.*
6 *She's usually very friendly.*
7 *He doesn't often wear jeans.*

2

Students add adverbs to the sentences to make them true for their own situation. The answers will depend on the individual student but check that the position of the adverbs is correct.

Language Summary 2

Refer back to Lesson 3 Activity 1, where these jobs were introduced.
Use the patterns in Language Summary 2 for oral practice with the four jobs given here and any other jobs the students know.

3

Exercise 3 extends the use of the indefinite article to other nouns introduced in Unit 1.

Answers

2 Emma is *an* art student.
3 Mike is *a* business student.
4 Pete hasn't got *a* television.
5 correct
6 I've got *a* blue car.
7 I haven't got *a* guitar.
8 correct
9 He's *a* good doctor.
10 correct
11 She's *an* independent student.

4

This exercise recycles the language from Lessons 1, 2 and 3.

Answers

Jane is 26 *years* old. She's got short *fair* hair and *blue* eyes. She *lives* on her own in Birmingham. She's got a good job – she's an *engineer*. She's an *independent* person and she likes going for walks on her own. In the *evening* she does a lot of sport. She doesn't like *discos* but she goes out to cafés with her *friends*.

The theme of this unit is dreams in the sense of *ideal* objects and situations. In the first two lessons, the students discuss 'dream' hotels and cars. The third lesson broadens the theme to include activities for a perfect day/weekend. In all three lessons students should be encouraged to be imaginative and not always be limited to what is realistic.

Lesson 1 *Dream hotel*

Aims: To discuss hotels and their facilities, and to introduce the use of *can* for possibility.

Language focus

can for possibility
You **can** do lots of sport.
You **can** play tennis.

Skills focus

- **Reading:** hotel brochures for specific information
- **Writing:** holiday postcards and an entry for a hotel brochure
- **Speaking:** discussing a dream hotel

Vocabulary focus

- Adjectives describing hotels: *cheap, good, friendly, great*
- Hotel facilities: *bar, fitness centre, restaurant, swimming pool*
- Holiday activities: *riding, walking, relaxing, shopping*
- Collocations of verbs and nouns
  Go swimming
  Watch television

Review

Use the profiles the students wrote about themselves for their homework to make a class profile. First get students to work in groups to make a summary of the information, eg *how many have the same job/are the same nationality, how many have fair/dark hair, how many have a cat/car, likes/dislikes*, etc. The simplest way to deal with this may be to have a heading for each topic and note down how many in each group do/like/have that item. The results can then be reported back to the class as a whole and noted on the board, eg *five people have fair hair; seven people have a cat; 12 people like discos*, etc.
You could make each group responsible for writing up one or two topics and putting the information in the wall display about the class or in the class magazine.

1

If your class all come from the same area you could begin by eliciting the names of some hotels in the area. Then take the role of a tourist and ask the students to advise you about hotels, using the questions in Activity 1. Alternatively, if you have a multi-national class, ask the students to work in pairs with a partner from a different country and to take turns asking and answering the questions, giving information about their home towns.

2

Ask the students to match the pictures and words. Check understanding and practise pronunciation and word stress.

Answers

2	*disco*	**3**	*bar*
4	*swimming pool*	**5**	*riding*
6	*restaurant*	**7**	*walking*
8	*tennis*	**9**	*television*

3

Tell the class they are going to read about two hotels to find out what you can do there. This is the first extended reading skills activity in the book. Encourage the students to try it without dictionaries at first, and to focus only on the information they need for the table. Do not read the text aloud at this stage – the students should read it silently.
Students check answers in pairs before general feedback. At this stage, deal with any specific vocabulary questions but do not go through the text word by word.
Finally, you could read the text aloud.

Answers

	Hill View	Vista
bar	✓	✓
disco		✓
walking	✓	
swimming pool	✓	✓
restaurant	✓	
fitness centre	✓	
tennis	✓	✓
riding	✓	
bedrooms with TV		✓
bedrooms with own bathrooms	✓	

4

You could do practice pages Exercises 1 and 2 (on collocations and activities that can and can't be done in different hotels) at this stage in preparation for the next writing activity.
Tell students to look at the photos in pairs and ask them which hotel Mario is probably staying at, and how they can tell. Introduce the idea of holiday postcards. Then elicit several possible ways to complete the postcard from Mario. Finally ask students to complete it on their own.

Answers

Mario is probably at the Vista hotel – he's by the sea.

Dear Emma

    I'm having a really good holiday here. The hotel is great. It's only 1 km from *the town centre* and a few metres from *the sea*. During the day I *go to the swimming pool/relax by the sea/by the swimming pool/go shopping in the town* and in the evening I *go to the bar/go to the disco* with some friends from the hotel.

Best wishes

Mario

5

Ask students to work in groups and to invent a 'dream hotel'. Encourage them to extend the ideas from the lesson, using dictionaries as necessary. If possible, provide large sheets of paper for the groups so that they can display their work. Circulate and help. This 'dream hotel' is the basis for the homework.

Homework

Tell students to use the postcard in Activity 4 as a model and to include an address on the right-hand side. The postcard is from the 'dream hotel' they discussed in their groups and so they should describe appropriate activities for that hotel.

Practice *page 69*

1

This is the first of a series of collocation exercises in which students match words often found together. The aim of these exercises is to stress the importance of learning vocabulary combinations rather than lists of isolated words.
After the students have done the exercise check it and elicit the difference in use and meaning between *go to* (a place) and *go/play/watch* (an activity). Ask students if they can remember any similar combinations from the lesson (eg *go walking/go to* the fitness centre/go shopping).

Answers

Go *riding/swimming*
Go *to the bathroom/the bar/the disco/the hotel/the restaurant*
Play *football/tennis*
Watch *television/football (on television)/tennis (on television)*

Language Summary

Refer the students back to Lesson 1 Activity 3.
Ask them to underline all the examples of *can* in the first text (the description of the Hill View Hotel). Relate this to the Language Summary. Note that only the use of *can* for possibility is included here.

2

This exercise practises *can/can't* together with the verb/noun collocations focused on in Exercise 1.

Answers

  2 *You can play tennis.*
  3 *You can't go riding.*
  4 *You can go to the restaurant.*
  5 *You can't go swimming.*
  6 *You can go to the fitness centre.*
  7 *You can go walking.*
  8 *You can go shopping.*

3

This extends the use of *can* to include questions, and short answers, and revises vocabulary from the lesson.

Answers

  2 *Can you play tennis there? Yes, you can.*
  3 *Can you go swimming there? Yes, you can.*
  4 *Can you go riding there? No, you can't.*
  5 *Can you play football there? Yes, you can.*

4

This activity practises the verbs *be* and *have got* from Unit 1, together with *can* from this lesson. It also provides a model dialogue for booking a hotel room, which could be used for speaking practice afterwards.

Answers

  Recep.: Hello. Holiday Hotel. *Can* I help you?
  Mike: Yes. *Have* you *got* a double room for 5th September, please?
  Recep.: One moment please … Yes, we *have*.
  Mike: Good. And *has* the hotel *got* a restaurant?
  Recep.: No, I'm afraid it *hasn't*, but the hotel *is* in the town centre. You *can* walk to lots of good restaurants.
  Mike: OK, good.
  Recep.: *Can* I have your name, please?
  Mike: Yes, it's Mike Green. Can I pay by credit card?
  Recep.: Yes, of course. One double room for September 5th.
  Mike: Thank you. Goodbye.

5

Introduce the concept of word stress. Then read the words aloud so that the students can match them to the correct patterns. This activity demonstrates the fact that most two-syllable words in English have the stress on the first syllable.

Answers

  ■ ■   disco bathroom bedroom centre fitness
               football riding swimming tennis
  ■ ■   hotel relax

Lesson 2 *Dream car*

Aims: To extend and practise the language of physical description, using cars as a topic.

Language focus

1 Adjectives with and without nouns
   It's **expensive**
   It's an **expensive car**

2 Prepositions: *in/at/during/to/on*
   I live **in** London.

Skills focus

- **Writing:** a description of an ideal car
- **Listening:** to short monologues for main idea and detail
- **Speaking:** describing a car

Vocabulary focus

- Adjectives collocating with *car: big, cheap, practical, safe*
- Other car vocabulary: *drive, park, stop*
- Colours: *black, red*

Review

If the posters with advertisements for the students' dream hotels from the last lesson are still displayed, you could use these as the basis for a matching activity. Collect the postcards the students wrote for their homework and read out some of the messages, asking the class to match them to the appropriate hotel description. After correction, all the postcards could be displayed next to the matching hotel descriptions.

Warmer

Bring in some pictures of unusual or luxury cars, or ask the students to bring some in.
If appropriate to the class, ask how many students can drive, and how many have cars. Elicit the types of cars owned by the students, or by their parents, what colour they are (this is a good opportunity to teach the colours in English), and any other details the students are able to give about their cars. You could also ask the class their opinions about the best cars made in their country, and in the world.

1

The vocabulary focus here is collocation of adjectives and nouns. Students copy the appropriate adjectives onto the diagram. Encourage them to add extra adjectives, eg colours. Check understanding of the vocabulary, using pictures and examples.

Possible answers

big cheap expensive fast good practical safe slow small, strong

2

Students could compare the adjectives they have chosen in pairs.

Possible answers

Picture above: Ferrari Testarossa – *fast expensive good*
Picture below: Jeep – *practical strong safe*

3

Students predict which is Jacky's dream car and which is Dominic's, using the text and photos as a guide. Encourage them to give reasons for their answers, but don't give the correct answers until after the listening.
▭ Play the cassette twice, the first time listening for the cars and the second time for the adjectives.

Answers

Jacky: Testarossa – *fast expensive good*
Dominic: Jeep – *practical strong safe*

When eliciting answers you could practise the pronunciation of the adjectives, first in isolation and then asking the students to produce sentences, eg *Jacky's dream car is fast/It's a fast car.* Practice page 70 Exercise 1 reinforces these two patterns and would fit in well here.

4

This activity extends the topic from existing cars to possible cars of the future. Ask students to read the text and identify the car. Discuss its features and introduce additional vocabulary as necessary (eg *wheels, windows*) when discussing the pictures.

Answer

The second picture

5

Students could describe either a real car or an imaginary one. Tell them they should describe its size, colour, and anything unusual about it, and say what it can do, where it can go, how fast it can go and why it is their dream car. Some students may also like to draw a picture of their dream car.

Homework

Students write about their dream car, again using a drawing or finding a picture to illustrate it if possible.

Practice *page 70*

Language Summary 1

Refer back to the pictures in Lesson 2 Activity 2.
Ask the students to make sentences about the cars. (See Teacher's notes for Activity 2.) Point out the use of the article with singular nouns such as *car*, and check that students understand why it is *a* cheap car but *an* expensive car. Give the students an example of the plural forms: they're *cheap* and they're *cheap* cars.

1

Exercise 1 gives practice in these points.

Answers

2 correct
3 Oxford is *a* big town.
4 correct
5 correct
6 correct
7 It's *a* friendly hotel.
8 He is *a* good engineer.
9 correct
10 The hotel has got *a* big swimming pool.

2

This extends the collocations of the adjectives from Exercise 1 to other nouns. Check that students understand that *two* adjectives are possible in each case.

Answers

The wrong adjectives are:

2 *clever*
3 *independent*
4 *strong*
5 *pretty*
6 *fast*
7 *clever*
8 *cheap*
9 *safe*

3

This exercise focuses on prepositions which the students have met in Units 1 and 2. Encourage them to learn prepositions in the context of examples such as those in Language Summary 2, as the system is probably different in their own language.

Answers

1 *in* Rome
2 *in* a big restaurant
3 *in* the centre of Rome
4 *on* his bike
5 *in* the evening
6 *at* night
7 *to* discos and cafés
8 *at* home
9 *on* his own.

4

In Exercise 4 students complete sentences giving true information about themselves.

Lesson 3 *Dream day*

Aims: To listen to other people's ideas of a perfect day, and then for the students to make plans for a perfect day/weekend of their own.

Language focus

1 *Want to* + verb
   I **want to** drive a Porsche.
   I **don't want to** go shopping.

2 Prepositions: *on, to, with*
   I want to travel **on** Concorde.
   I want to go **to** bed **with** a good book.

Skills focus

- **Listening:** for the main idea and detail
- **Speaking:** discussing ideas for a perfect weekend
- **Writing:** a weekend plan

Vocabulary focus

- People to meet: *my favourite filmstar, the national football team*
- Things to see: *the Pyramids, the Great Wall of China, a Caribbean beach, dinosaurs*
- Things to do: *relax, drive, go to..., go back in time, buy, win, meet, see, fly, take part in*
- Days and times of day: *Saturday, Sunday, morning, afternoon, evening*

Review

Take in the homework (descriptions of 'dream cars') to mark. Revise adjectives from Unit 2 Lessons 1 and 2. Give students nouns such as *hotel, restaurant, bar, swimming pool, disco, town, car, motorbike, student, teacher*, etc and quickly ask them to suggest a possible adjective for each one, eg a *cheap* hotel/a *big* restaurant/a *friendly* bar, etc.

1

Students number the sentences individually. They then walk around and try to find someone else who has chosen the same order as them. Finally with that person they decide on one more thing they would both like to do.

2

Give the students time to look at the pictures. Then play the cassette and ask them to match the pictures to the people.

Answers

2 *Rachel – 5*	**3** *Ben – 4*
4 *Mike – 1*	**5** *Jacky – 2*

3

Tell students to look at the sentences and fill in any words they can remember before playing the cassette again.
After checking the answers, ask students to decide whose dream day they like best.

Answers

2 *Disneyworld*
3 *drive*
4 *clothes*
5 *time*
6 *see*
7 *Games*
8 *medal*
9 *go*
10 *book*

4

Students classify the 'Dream day' activities into groups. They then think of more activities themselves. Remind them that this is a *dream* day – they have unlimited money, and can travel to the past or the future.

Answers

People to meet:	**2**	*Tom Cruise*
	8	*the national football team*
Places to see:	**3**	*Copacabana beach in Brazil*
	7	*The Great Wall of China*
Things to do:	**1**	*A trip on Concorde*
	4	*play football for your country*
	5	*go to an expensive restaurant in Paris*
	6	*drive a Porsche*

Practice page 71 Exercise 4 may be useful for more ideas here.

5

For this activity the students work in groups to plan a dream weekend with six activities.

6

Each group reports back to the class about their dream weekend, using the structure given in the speech bubble (*On ... we want to ...*). The class could then decide which group has the most enjoyable/most unusual weekend.

Homework

This consolidates the topic of the unit and extends it to the students' own lives, giving further practice of *I want to/I don't want to*.

Practice *page 71*

1

Although the lesson mainly focuses on the affirmative form *I **want to***, the negative form also occurs. (See the example in Lesson 3 Activity 5.)
For Exercise 1, emphasize that *only* the words in the box should be used to make sentences, but the words can be used over and over again. At least sixteen sentences are possible, eight with *there* and eight without.

Answers

1 *She wants to go (there).*
2 *She wants to drive (there).*
3 *She doesn't want to go (there).*
4 *She doesn't want to drive (there).*
5 *I want to go (there).*
6 *I don't want to go (there).*
7 *I want to drive (there).*
8 *I don't want to drive (there).*

2

This gives further practice in using the affirmative and negative forms of *want to*. Like the homework for Lesson 3, it demands a personal response but it is controlled rather than creative.
Answers depend on the students.

3

This revises and extends the use of some of the prepositions met in the unit. Encourage students to keep records of prepositions with examples. You may also like to make a wall display which can be referred to, and added to, during the course.

Answers

1 *On* Sundays I usually go *to* a football match *with* Pepe.
2 *On* Saturdays Sonya usually goes *to* work.
3 This evening I want to stay at home *with* a good book.
4 I sometimes go *to* a café *with* my friends in the evening.
5 *On* Saturday mornings I go *to* town and do the shopping.
6 You can go *to* the swimming pool *on* Sundays.

4

This reviews some of the vocabulary from Lesson 3 and also gives further practice with *I want to ...*

Answers

2 *I want to drive an Alfa Romeo.*
3 *I want to win a medal.*
4 *I want to meet Alain Prost.*
5 *I want to fly on Concorde.*
6 *I want to sleep all weekend.*
7 *I want to live in a big town.*
8 *I want to be happy.*

5

The word square revises verbs from Lesson 3. You could do this as a competition.

Answers

Across: *win play live drive like have*
Down: *work be go sleep meet fly stay*

The theme of this unit is leisure and recreation, focusing on music, sport and computer games. Students learn how to express their feelings and how to report on what they see and experience.

Lesson 1 *I like music*

Aims: To express feelings about kinds of music, animals, sport and entertainment, and to find out how other people feel about them.

Language focus

1 Talking about likes and dislikes
I **like** it a lot.
I **don't mind** reggae.
I **don't like** it at all.

2 Question forms with *What* and *How*
What do you call this sort of music?
How do you feel about jazz?

Skills focus

- **Listening:** to a conversation to get the main idea; for information to complete notes on language used
- **Speaking:** expressing feelings; carrying out a class survey and reporting the results from notes
- **Writing:** taking notes and writing up a brief report of a survey

Vocabulary focus

- Music: *classical, jazz, heavy metal, disco, reggae*
- Animals: *cats, dogs, snakes, spiders*
- Entertainment: *cinemas, discos, opera, TV*
- Sport: *football, opera, skiing, swimming*

Review

Ask students to read, compare and check their homework 'My dream life' together. You could also display the homework or read out different versions and ask the students to guess who the authors are.

Warmer

- Ask a couple of students to come to the board and write the names of some English or American singers/groups they enjoy listening to. Other students can help with ideas or spelling. (This is preferable to writing students' suggestions up yourself as some of the names may be quite strange and the students will probably be more familiar with them than you are.)

1

Play the first part of the cassette through once. Students work alone noting the order in which they hear the music. Then they compare their answers. Play the cassette again, if necessary.

Answers

1 *jazz*   2 *disco*   3 *classical* 4 *reggae*   5 *heavy metal*

2

Write the table on the board and check that the students understand the task. Play the cassette through once. Students complete their tables as they listen. They then compare answers. Finally one student writes them on the board.

Answers

		😀	😐	🙁
disco music	Helen	✓		
	Phil			✓
classical music	Helen	✓		
	Phil			✓
reggae	Helen		✓	
	Phil		✓	
jazz	Helen			✓
	Phil		✓	
heavy metal	Helen	✓		
	Phil	✓		

3

Focus the students' attention on the gaps in the table and play the cassette again. Then play it again, stopping after each expression for them to complete the table.
Extend the table with more suggestions from the students, eg *really good, brilliant, cool, awful, terrible, boring, I hate/adore it.* Emphasize the importance of stress and intonation, using the cassette as a model where possible. Note the unenthusiastic sentence stress and intonation in *I don't mind reggae* and *I'm not very keen on it.*

Answers

How do you feel about disco music?

😀	😐	🙁
It's *great!*	It's *OK.*	I don't *like* it at all.
I *like* it a lot.	I don't *mind* it.	I'm *not* very
I *love* it!	It's *alright.*	*keen* on it.

4

Elicit any other types of music the students are interested in and write them on the board. Then get them to work in pairs and ask their partner how they feel about the music types from Activity 1 and the additional ones they suggested. Practice page 72 Exercise 2 could be done here as written consolidation.

5

Ask students to work in groups of three or four to match the words and topics in the word map. You may also want to elicit more topics and vocabulary, eg cars, food/drink, school subjects (with younger students), politicians (with adults).

Answers

Animals:	*horses, snakes, spiders*
Sport:	*cycling, football, skiing, swimming*
Entertainment:	*the cinema, opera, pop concerts, TV*

6

Ask each student to choose a topic and fill in their survey form. Tell students from one group to interview another group or walk around the class at random. They should put a tick for each answer in the appropriate column. If necessary write up a model:
How do you feel about cats?
I love them.

7

Practise the language in the table with the class, eliciting single sentences from different students. Do not focus on the past form *interviewed* at this stage, but check that the students can use the correct forms for singular and plural (*one person .../two people ...*). Then ask students to compare their survey reports in pairs, making sure they talk to someone with a different topic. After that get them to form new pairs and discuss their surveys again.
Finally, as preparation for the homework, ask one or two students to report their survey results to the whole class.

Homework

Ask students to write their survey results in the form of a paragraph of about 50 words, using the table in Activity 7 to help them.
This could be extended by asking the students to survey their family and friends at home (in their own language if necessary) and write a survey report in English.

Practice *page 72*

Language Summary

Look at the examples given in the Language Summary. Check that students understand the meanings. (They are arranged on a scale from the most positive to the most negative.) Do some oral practice to check that the students can cope with the forms (eg, use of *-s* with present simple, use of the verb *be* with **not very keen on**, use of the negative **doesn't/don't** forms).

1

Then ask students to do the first activity.

Answers

2 He loves *classical music/Mozart.*
3 She isn't very keen on *babies.*
4 She doesn't mind *spiders.*
5 He doesn't like *snakes* at all.
6 She likes *tennis* a lot.

As a follow-up the students could give their own feelings about the same things.

2

Here the students need not be restricted to the five types of music given in the lesson.

3

The use of *what* and *how* is likely to be different in the students' own language. Encourage them to learn *What do you call...* and *How do you spell...* as set phrases, since these are likely to recur frequently in the classroom.

Answers

2 *What do you like doing?*
3 *What sort of clothes do you like?*
4 *How do you spell 'independent'?*
5 *What sort of car have you got?*
6 *How do you get to Peter's house?*

4

This can be done orally with the whole class at first. When the exercise has been done and the answers checked, the dialogues could be practised by students in pairs, paying particular attention to stress and intonation.

Answers

1 A: *What* do you call this sort of music?
   A: Oh. *How* do you spell reggae?
   A: *How* do you feel about this sort of music?
2 A: Excuse me. *What's* your name?
   A: And *what* do you do?
   A: *What* are you studying?
   A: *How* do you get to College in the morning?

5

After doing this the students could make up further examples for themselves.

Answers

2 *cats (all the others are entertainments)*
3 *football (all the others are alive)*
4 *music (all the others are sports)*
5 *hotel (all the others are types of transport)*
6 *jogging (all the others are machines)*

Lesson 2 *Sports crazy*

Aims: To practise and extend the language of likes and dislikes in the context of sport.

Language focus

1 *I like* + *-ing*
like + noun
Which sports do you **like watching**?
I **like football**.

2 Collocation of verbs and nouns (sports vocabulary)
To *do* aerobics.
To *play* basketball.
To *go* jogging

Skills focus

- **Reading:** a newspaper article to get the main idea; to answer questions on detail and to focus on the order of information within a text
- **Listening:** to a range of short dialogues to identify the main topics and specific language items (verb/noun collocations)

Vocabulary focus

- Revision of sports: *football, swimming, tennis, skiing*
- Extension of sports vocabulary: *aerobics, basketball, cricket, gymnastics, golf, jogging, volleyball*
- General sports language: *team, support, supporter, match*

Review

Ask students to exchange the surveys they wrote for homework. Encourage peer correction, particularly of present tense verbs (*like/likes, doesn't mind/don't mind*, etc). Display corrected surveys on the notice board if possible.

Warmer

With Student's Books closed, elicit the sports from Activity 1 using pictures or mime. Practise pronunciation and word stress, especially aer*o*bics, gym*n*astics.

1

Play the cassette through once. Students work alone noting the order of the sports. Ask students to compare answers in pairs.

Answers

2 *swimming*		**3** *cricket*		**4** *gymnastics*	
5 *football*		**6** *aerobics*		**7** *golf*	
8 *skiing*		**9** *basketball*		**10** *tennis*	
11 *volleyball*					

2

Play the first short dialogue again and focus on the verb used with *jogging* (*go*). Ask students to work in pairs and predict which verbs go with the other sports. Then play the complete section so the students can check their predictions. Play it again if necessary.

Answers

play: *basketball, cricket, football, golf, tennis, volleyball*
go: *jogging, skiing, swimming*
do: *aerobics, gymnastics*

Practice page 72 Exercise 3 could also be done at this stage.

3

Ask students to work in small groups and discuss the questions. Monitor for correct use of the *-ing* form of the verb after *like*. Find out if a special team or player is particularly popular with the class.
Practice page 72 Exercise 2 would fit in well here.

4

Focus the students' attention on the picture of Ann Crossley. Ask them to guess where she comes from.
Look at the pre-reading questions with students and encourage them to read quickly for this information only.

Answers

1 *football*	**2** *watch it*	**3** *yes*	**4** *yes*

5

Ask the students to read a second time to answer these more detailed questions. Deal with any vocabulary problems.

Answers

1 *Yes.*
2 *They don't like it.*
3 *It's the most important thing in her life.*
4 *She dyes it red, white and blue.*

6

This activity focuses on the order of the information within the text. When checking the answers, ask students for the main information about each topic to prepare for the next activity, eg 'Number 1 was Ann's age. How old is she?' (58)

Answers

2 the team Ann supports
3 Ann's first match
4 the places Ann goes to
5 Ann's family
6 the most important thing in Ann's life
7 the colours Ann wears at matches

7

Tell the students to work in pairs and cover the reading text. Ask them to say as much as they can about Ann, using the topics in Activity 6 to help them.

Homework

This could be extended by asking the students to write another paragraph about someone in their class or family who likes sport.

Answers

Ann follows her football *team* to every *match*. She wears *blue* clothes and dyes her hair *blue*, or red, *white* and *blue*. She is *58* years old, but *football* is the most *important* thing in her *life*.

The topic of this lesson could be extended by organizing a class project on a particular team or player, with students collecting pictures and writing information in English for a classroom display.

Practice *page 73*

1

Refer students to Lesson 2 Activity 3. Highlight Language Summary 1.
Introduce Ann's husband and elicit some sentences orally from the pictures.
Students complete the exercise alone.

Answers

2 *He likes (watching) television.*
3 *He doesn't like swimming.*
4 *He doesn't like (playing) tennis.*
5 *He doesn't mind walking.*
6 *He doesn't mind reading.*
7 *He doesn't like shopping.*
8 *He likes (playing) golf.*

2

Students may be able to remember information about someone in their group from Lesson 2 Activity 3. Otherwise, give time for them to interview one another in pairs before completing the sentences.
Check that they are using the appropriate first and third person verb forms when writing.

3

Refer students back to Lesson 2 Activity 2. Look at the Language Summary together.
Ask students to complete the exercise alone and check in pairs.

Answers

2 *play*
3 *do*
4 *do*
5 *play*
6 *go*
7 *play*
8 *go*

4

Ask students to complete the exercise.
This could be extended by games of Hangman played in pairs or groups.

Answers

jogging	*swimming*	*tennis*	*skiing*	*gymnastics*
basketball	*cricket*	*golf*	*aerobics*	*volleyball*

5

Ask students to do the exercise in pairs.

Answers

ball: *football, tennis, basketball, cricket, golf, volleyball*
team games: *football, basketball, cricket, volleyball*

Extend this by encouraging students to add other sports.

Lesson 3 *Almost real*

Aims: To introduce the present continuous used to report events happening at the time of speaking. The context for this lesson is the recent computer development which allows the user to enter a three-dimensional 'computer world' and move around in it. (This is known as 'virtual reality' – some students may have come across it in games or heard about it.)

Language focus

1 Present continuous: *be + -ing*
   The curtains **are opening**.
   I**'m going** through the door.

2 Location and direction
   What's **in front of** you?
   Now turn your head **to the left**.

Skills focus

- **Listening:** to a conversation to order the main events and to identify specific language items
- **Speaking:** describing events in a story
- **Reading:** instructions to label a diagram

Vocabulary focus

- Language of computer games: *computer, handset, buttons, helmet*
- Inside a room: *door, window, curtains, wall, picture*
- The sea: *fish, sea, ship*
- Activity verbs: *come, go, turn, get, press, look*

Review

Ask the students what they remember about Ann Crossley (Unit 3 Lesson 2) and check the homework.
Revise the names of the sports quickly and use these to lead on to the topic of hobbies.
Ask the students what else they like doing in their free time besides sport. Find out if any students play computer games or have computers at home.

1

Ask the students to look at Activity 1 and discuss it in pairs. Ask several pairs how they feel. If a lot of the class are interested in computer games, they could tell you the names of the games they know.

2

Focus students' attention on the picture. Explain that this is a special type of computer game. Students read the text and label the diagram.

Answers

> From top to bottom:
> *helmet*
> *buttons*
> *handset*
> *computer*

3

Pre-teach vocabulary: *room, door, window, curtains, wall, picture*, using the classroom and the picture in Activity 3. Use the classroom situation and the same vocabulary to teach *in front of/behind/left/right*. and to check understanding of 'There's'. Focus on understanding at this stage rather than production. Ask students to match the questions and answers.
Play the cassette for students to check the answers. After this the students could practise the dialogue in pairs, with Mike making appropriate movements.

Answers

> *A window, with curtains.*
> *There's a picture on the wall.*
> *There's a door.*

4

Focus the students' attention on the seven pictures and tell them that this is what Mike sees next. Use the pictures to teach the vocabulary: *fish, bird, sea, ship*. Ask the students to work in pairs and predict the order of the pictures. Then play the cassette and ask the students to number the pictures.

Answers

Order of pictures:

5

Ask the students to tell you the first part of the story (pictures 1, 2, 3). If they have difficulty, you could play the first part of the cassette again (ending at '*... now I'm going away from the window*').
Tell the students to read the last part of the story and look at the words in the box. Then play the second part of the cassette so that the students can complete the text.

Answers

2 *getting*	**3** *going*	**4** *coming*
5 *pressing*	**6** *going*	**7** *turning*

When checking these answers, focus on the seven examples of the present continuous. Ask the students *when* the events are happening (now) and look at the form of the verb.
Note Here short forms are used with pronouns, eg *I, it* and full forms with nouns, eg *sea.*
Practice page 74 Exercises 1 and 2 would fit in well here.

6

In this activity the students visualize what happens when they go through a door into another part of the game. Ask the students to work in groups and invent their own story. Encourage them to be creative and also to use the present continuous. Help them with vocabulary as necessary.

7

Ask each student to find a partner from another group and tell each other their stories.
If you don't think your class could cope with Activities 6 and 7 in groups, you could elicit a story from the whole class together and build this up on the blackboard.
Then ask the students to think of an ending to the story for homework.

Homework

Students might like to illustrate their story with a picture or prepare a sequence of pictures with commentary for a class display.

Practice *page 74*

1

Refer students to Lesson 3 Activity 5.
Focus on the form and use of the present continuous. (See Teacher's notes on Activity 5.) Students complete Exercise 1.

Answers

go	going
look	*looking*
open	opening
press	*pressing*
turn	turning
come	*coming*
put	putting
get	*getting*

After checking the answers, encourage students to look for rules for forming the *-ing* form of the verb. (Most verbs add *-ing* to the infinitive form, but verbs ending in *-e* drop the *-e* (eg *come*), and verbs with a short vowel followed by a single consonant double the last consonant (eg *put*).) Students could add any other verbs they know to this chart.

2

This exercise also focuses on form, giving practice with the short form of the verb. Ask the students to complete it alone. Then check the verb forms. If necessary, tell the students to cover the passage, and check the spelling of the *-ing* forms.

Answers

2 *are*	**3** *is*	**4** *is/'s*	**5** *am/'m*

3

This exercise focuses on use. Revise the use of the present simple for habits and regular activities and contrast this with the use of the present continuous for events at or around the time of speaking. Establish the idea of present simple for permanent states or long-term habits contrasted with present continuous for short-term situations.
Ask the students to do the exercise alone and then check the answers in pairs.

Answers

I start	*I don't finish*	*I'm doing*
I'm learning	*I'm not working*	*I'm having*

4

Refer back to the expressions of location and direction in Lesson 3 Activity 3.
(Remember that the emphasis here is on recognition and not production. We would not expect students to use the various prepositions accurately at this stage, eg *to* the left/*on* the left.)
Ask students to find the mistakes in the text and correct them. They could do this in pairs.

Answers

The man is *in front of* the window, looking at the cat. The cat is going *up* the tree. The fish is on the man's *left* and the dog is on his *right*. The baby is behind the man and it is going *towards* the dog.

This could be followed by a picture dictation, where the teacher describes a simple picture and the students draw it, eg: '*Draw a hotel with two doors and six windows. In front of the hotel there is a big car, with a woman sitting in it. On the left of the hotel there is a swimming pool, with two boys in it. On the right of the car there is a man with a dog. There is a bird in the sky. How many people are there in your picture?'* (*four*)

The theme of this unit is communication – what we talk about, who we talk to, and how we do it.

Lesson 1 *Nice to meet you*

Aims: To present students with features of conversation and to introduce them to strategies for beginning and continuing conversations.

Language focus

1 Questions with question tags
  The music's good, **isn't it**?
  You're a friend of Jim's, **aren't you**?

2 *Can* for requests
  Can I have a look?
  Can you give me his phone number?

Skills focus

- **Listening:** to conversations for the main idea and detail
- **Speaking:** starting and continuing conversations

Vocabulary focus

- **Places where you meet people:** *disco, conference, party*
- **Topics of conversation:** *food, clothes, friends, cars*
- **Adjectives expressing opinions:** *difficult, good, crowded, delicious, great, nice*

Review

Collect or display the computer story homework from Unit 3 Lesson 3.

1

Ask students to suggest some places in their town where you can go to meet people.
Elicit two or three. Then ask the students to look at the word square and find the eight places hidden there.

Answers

Across: *disco, restaurant, work*
Down: *party, café, club, bar, hotel*

2

Ask students to read through the questions and answers and match them.
Ask students to work in pairs to decide where the conversations might take place, matching them to the places in the word square.
Note: There are several possible answers for some of the conversations.

Answers

2 e	3 b	4 a	5 c

1 *d: conference or work*
2 *e: disco, party or club*
3 *b: hotel*
4 *a: restaurant, café or hotel*
5 *c: party – or maybe club/disco*

3

Tell the students they are going to listen to another conversation. Give them time to read the four sentences and then play the cassette.

Answers

1 *false*	3 *false*
2 *true*	4 *false*

4

Play the cassette again so that students can number the phrases they hear in the correct order. Point out how the two speakers keep the conversation going – ie by saying more than just *yes* or *no* in reply to a question, and by using question tags.
Look at the formation of one type of tag – *It is ... isn't it*, and elicit the general rule.
(The tag is added to the end of the statement. It is formed by the appropriate form of *be, do* or *have* followed by a pronoun referring to the subject of the sentence. Modals are not introduced at this stage and only negative tags are practised.)
Play the cassette again and ask the students to listen to the intonation pattern.
Note All the question tags in this lesson are falling not rising as the questions are expecting agreement rather than asking for new information.

Answers

2 Yes, of course.	4 It's quite difficult, isn't it?
3 Sure.	5 Yes it is, isn't it?

Practice page 75 Exercises 1 and 2 could be done here for further reinforcement and extension of question tags.

5

Ask students to read the conversations and complete them.

Answers

1 Where's Mary? Is she here?
  No, she's away on business.
  Oh, where is she? Anywhere interesting?
2 How's your new car?
  Oh, it's great. I really like driving it.
  It's a BMW, isn't it?

3 You look nice. Is that sweater new?
Yes. Do you like it?
Yes, the colour really suits you.
4 You're a friend of Jim's, aren't you?
That's right, he lives next door to me.
Can you give me his phone number? I haven't got it.
Yes, of course. It's 52247.

6

Ask the students to work in pairs. They choose a conversation and practise it, extending it for a few more lines. Remind them about the falling intonation pattern of this type of question tag. Circulate and help students as necessary.
Ask several pairs to read their conversation, acting it out from memory if possible.
An extension activity for this lesson would be a 'find your partners' mingle where the lines of the dialogues from Activities 2, 4 and 5 are written on separate strips of paper and distributed to the students. (The number of lines selected will depend on the number of students in the class.) Each student learns his or her line by heart and then circulates, repeating the line to find people with the other lines of their conversation. Finally, each pair or group performs their conversation.

Homework

Activity 6 was preparation for the homework. Tell students that they should be ready to read their conversation in class with a partner.

Practice *page 75*

Language Summary 1

Question tags are introduced early as they are such an important feature of spoken English. They are most often used when the listener is expected to agree with the speaker. In this case the tag has a falling intonation, eg *isn't it*.

1

This relates to Activity 4, and focuses only on question tags with the verb *be*, where the main part of the sentence is affirmative and the tag is negative. Point out the irregular tag *I am ... aren't I*.

Answers

2 They're in the restaurant, *aren't they.*
3 You're from Turkey, *aren't you?*
4 She's away on business, *isn't she?*
5 I'm first, *aren't I?*
6 We're last, *aren't we?*

2

This extends the use of question tags to include other verbs in the present simple. As in Exercise 1, the emphasis is on recognition rather than on production. Students need information from Unit 1, Lesson 1 to complete this exercise.

Answers

2 *He's got a motorbike, hasn't he?*
3 *He plays the guitar, doesn't he?*
4 *He hasn't got a car, has he?*
5 *He doesn't speak Italian, does he?*
6 *He's 26, isn't he?*

2 *Yes, he has*   **3** *Yes, he does*
4 *No, he hasn't*   **5** *No, he doesn't*
6 *No, he isn't. (He's 22.)*

3

Here the students produce question tags to complete a conversation. You could go through the conversation with them, checking understanding and eliciting the answers orally before they write it.

Answers

B: You go to the sports centre, *don't you?*
A: You do aerobics, *don't you?*
B: She teaches jazz-dance too, *doesn't she?*
A: You've got a daughter too, *haven't you?*
B: It's a difficult age, *isn't it?*

4

The students met the use of *can* for possibility in Unit 2 Lesson 1 (Dream hotel). Here they meet the use of *can* for requests.

Answers

2 *have*   **3** *borrow*   **4** *give*   **5** *tell*   **6** *meet*

After checking this exercise you could ask the students to think of other requests they might use in the classroom.

5

Students match the requests with the answers. These include some very common requests with **can** and useful responses.

Answers

2 *e*   **3** *a*   **4** *c*   **5** *d*

The students then match the conversations to the places.

Answers

At a school 5   At home 3   In the street 5
In a shop 2   In a restaurant 4

Finally, students could think of other possible requests and answers for these places. When they act them out, the class could guess the place.

Lesson 2 *Get in touch*

Aims: To practise communicating over the telephone and expressing future plans.

Language focus

1 Present continuous for future plans, and future time expressions.
   I**'m moving** to Manchester soon.
   He**'s coming** to Oxford in next month.

2 Clauses of purpose with the infinitive
   I **use it to** send letters and pictures to New York.
   I **use it to** find and store information and to write letters.

3 Numbers: telephone numbers, prices, and ages

Skills focus

- **Listening:** to descriptions to identify objects and listening to recorded messages for the main idea and details
- **Writing:** an advertisement and replying to one
- **Reading:** short magazine advertisements for specific information
- **Speaking:** saying telephone numbers

Vocabulary focus

- Communication technology: *telephone, letter, fax, computer, answerphone, mobile phone*
- Travel: *sunshine, move, host family, bed, breakfast and evening meal, chalet, English course*
- Household equipment: *corkscrew, vacuum cleaner, keys*

Review

Check the written conversations done for homework for Unit 4 Lesson 1. Or do the suggested extension activity (see Lesson 1 Activity 6).

1

After the students have discussed the questions, do a quick class feedback. You could do a quick class survey on the blackboard.

2

Ask students to look at the picture of Rachel and discuss the questions as a class.

Answer

1 *1990s – because of the technology.*

Encourage the students to match the words to the pictures and help them with pronunciation and word stress. Discuss what these machines are used for in preparation for the next activity.

Answers

1 *portable computer*   2 *fax machine*
3 *answerphone*   4 *mobile phone*

3

Listen to the first part of the cassette and look at the example. Highlight the key words (*send/letters/pictures*) and stress that the students are listening for the main idea only. Play the rest of the cassette for the students to identify the machines, repeating if necessary.

Answers

2 *portable computer*
3 *mobile phone*
4 *answerphone*

You could follow this up by asking why Rachel needs each thing. Point out the structure *I use it to* + verb. Practice page 76 Exercise 3 could also be done at this stage, and would help students with the homework for the lesson.

4

Elicit the types of advertisements found in magazines. If necessary, point out that these may include personal advertisements. Ask students to read the three advertisements and answer the questions. They should compare answers in pairs afterwards. Make sure that the students understand the vocabulary and situations, as these are developed in the next two activities.

Answers

1 *July and August*   2 *bass guitar*
3 *No (He's moving there soon.)*   4 *Spain*
5 *No (He's coming next month.)*   6 *Alex's*

5

Explain the situation: one person answered each advertisement by phone. In each case they left a message on the answerphone as no-one was at home.
Play the three recorded messages and ask the students to write who each message was for.

Answers

Message 1 – *for Alex (second advertisement)*
Message 2 – *for Jane (third advertisement)*
Message 3 – *for Contact Agency (first advertisement)*

6

🔊 Ask the students to read through the sentences and then play the cassette again.

Answers

1 *true*
2 *true*
3 *false (She's starting in September.)*
4 *false (five - two parents and three children)*
5 *false (£65 a week)*

This activity could be followed by a discussion of the use of the present continuous for future plans, and Practice page 76 Exercise 1 could also be used at this stage. (See Teacher's notes for Practice page 76 Exercise 1.)

7

Encourage the students to use the advertisements in Activity 4 as models. Practice page 76 Exercise 1 also provides a good model for part 2 of this activity. Circulate and help as necessary.
Make sure students produce a final version of their advertisement that is clear and legible.

8

Tell students to exchange their advertisements with another pair. They then either plan a message or write a short letter in reply. If tape recorders are available students could record their messages. Provide a simple lay-out plan for letters if necessary. (A model is given on Practice page 76 Exercise 1.)

Homework

It will be useful to do Practice page 76 Exercises 3 and 4 to help students prepare for the homework.

Practice *page 76*

Language Summary 1

Refer back to Lesson 2 Activity 4
Ask the students to underline all the examples of the present continuous (there are four). Then ask them whether these refer to the present or the future. (All examples refer to the future except for *A Spanish student is looking for an English host family.*) Ask how they know that the future is being referred to and elicit the different time references that give this information. Establish that the present continuous can be used for future plans, but that we nearly always state the time being referred to in order to avoid confusion.

1

Students now complete the exercise.

Answers

2 *I'm moving - next October*
3 *I'm coming - next week*
4 *I'm waiting - now*

2

Lesson 2 includes quite a lot of work with numbers, and this activity practises the way telephone numbers are spoken. If this is done orally you could also get the students to practise the typical pauses used in speaking telephone numbers. (Usually the numbers are pronounced with a slight pause after each three numbers, eg five nine one, zero two five.)
Note In British English zero can also be pronounced /əʊ/.

591025 - five *nine* one, zero two five
69411 - six nine four *double one* (*one one*)
523569 - five two three, *five six* nine
872645 - eight seven two, six *four five*
988970 - nine *double eight*, nine seven zero

Language Summary 2

Refer the students to Lesson 2 Activity 3.
🔊 Play the cassette again if necessary or photocopy the tapescript. Establish the use of the infinitive with *to* to express purpose.

3

Ask the students to match the beginnings and endings of the sentences.

Answers

2 *I use my personal computer to write letters.*
3 *I use the fax machine to send letters quickly.*
4 *I use the photocopier to make copies of important papers.*
5 *I use the cassette recorder to play cassettes.*

4

This activity further extends the use of the infinitive of purpose for explaining the use of everyday objects. It is useful preparation for the homework for Lesson 2 and students could be asked to do this exercise before they do the homework.

Answers

2 *corkscrew – picture 4*
3 *contact lenses – picture 1*
4 *wallet – picture 2*
5 *vacuum cleaner – picture 3*

Lesson 3 *Can you talk about it?*

Aim: To continue the theme of communication in the context of talking about personal problems.

Language focus

1 Revision of question words *Who, What,* etc
   Who is he talking to?
   What do you talk about?

2 Possessive adjectives *my, his, her*
   My sister is interested in politics.
   Mike talks to people in **his** family about politics.

3 Prepositions after verbs: *to, about*
   Who do you talk **to about** politics?

Skills focus

- **Listening:** to a conversation and interviews to identify topics and people
- **Speaking:** interviewing people

Vocabulary focus

- Relationships: *mother, father, sister, brother, friends, boss, doctor*
- Topics of conversation: *money, the past, health, relationships, politics, films*

Review

Play Hangman with the names of objects from Unit 4 Lesson 2, eg keys, wallet.
Check the homework.

1

Use the picture to introduce the topic. Ask *where* the women are (in a café or a garden) and elicit suggestions on what they are talking about.
Then tell the students they are going to listen to a *different* conversation and give them time to read through the questions.
Play the cassette once and discuss possible answers. Play it again to check.

Answers

  1 *b*
  2 *c*
  3 *b*

2

This presents some of the topics that are common in conversations and prepares students for the listening and speaking activities later in the lesson.

Answers

  2 *politics*   **3** *health*   **4** *relationships*   **5** *money*

You could ask students to choose one of the sentences and think of a reply.

3

Before doing this activity, teach the vocabulary of family and relationships given in the Vocabulary focus. Students will need this, together with the topics from Activity 2.

4

Tell students they are going to hear Mike and Emma telling the interviewer who they talk to about the different topics listed.
Play Mike's interview first and give time for students to compare answers before listening to Emma.

Answers

	Mike	Emma
politics	*sister*	*family*
the past	*no-one*	*friends*
money	anybody/everybody	*people at college*
relationships	*close friends*	*brother*
health	*mum*	*doctor*

5

Prepare students for the writing by eliciting sentences orally using the table in Activity 4.

Answers

1 *politics, money and health*   2 *politics and relationships*
3 *money and relationships*   4 *the past*

6

This is a survey similar to the one in Unit 3 Lesson 1, but this time students work individually. Encourage them to think of different topics related to their own lives and interests. They then interview two other students and note down their answers. You may need to practise the question *Who do you talk to about ...?* before they begin.

Homework

This is a written consolidation of the survey, on the same model as the sentences in Activity 5.

Practice *page 77*

1

Remind students of the questions in Lesson 3 Activity 1. Elicit other question words, eg *how/when*.

Do some oral practice with the class to check that they are using these words correctly.
Then students do Exercise 1.

Answers

2 *Who* do you talk to when you have a problem?
3 *What* does Mike talk to his friends about?
4 *Where* does Mike live?
5 *Who* do you talk to about politics?

2

This is question formation practice based on the two questions that featured in the lesson.
Tell students to use the answers given to help them.

Answers

2 *What does Mike talk to his mother about?*
3 *Who does Emma talk to about health?*
4 *What does Emma talk to her brother about?*

3

The students met a similar exercise in Unit 2, Lesson 3 (Practice page 71, Exercise 1). Remind them that they can use only words from the box, but they do not have to use them all in any one sentence. Go through the example with the class, if necessary, drawing attention to the word order. Check the answers with the class, or let them check them in pairs.

Answers

1 *What do you do?*   2 *What is he doing?*
3 *What does he do?*   4 *What do you like?*
5 *What does he like?*   6 *Where are you going?*
7 *Where is he going?*   8 *Where is he?*
9 *Where are you*   10 *Is he going?*
11 *Are you going?*   12 *What is he?*
13 *What are you?*

Language Summary 2

Language Summary 2 focuses on possessive adjectives. These may cause problems for students if the system is different in their own language. Point out that the possessive adjective tells us who the noun belongs to, eg we say *his mother* for Mark's mother but *her mother* for Emma's mother.

4

Exercise 3 asks students to recognize the correct possessive forms.

Answers

His wife   *their son*   *their two daughters*
their son   *her nephew*

If you would like to do a productive exercise, students could talk about their own family or their partner's family in order to practise possessive adjectives.

5

Focus on the difference between the prepositions *to* and *about*, which came in the questions in Lesson 3 (Activity 1 onwards).

Answers

2 I'm phoning you *about* your advertisement.
3 I'm writing *to* you *about* your new job.
4 What is he phoning *about*?
5 I can't talk *about* that.
6 I don't like talking *about* politics.
7 I want to tell you *about* him.
8 She's speaking *to* her mother on the phone.
('*about*' her mother is also possible here, but less likely in this context)

The theme of this unit is first-time experiences, including childhood memories, first jobs and people who have done something for the first time at an early age.
Students practise talking about past events as well as comparing their lives then and now.

Lesson 1 *Can you remember?*

Aim: To introduce the past simple tense for completed events at a known time in the past.

Language focus

1 Past simple of regular and irregular verbs – affirmative and interrogative
In 1990 Roberto **was** in a road accident.
I **looked** through the classroom window.
The teacher **saw** me.
When **did** it happen?

2 Time references
When I was about fifteen, I took my brother's bicycle.
In 1986 I left college.

Skills focus

- **Reading:** short narratives for the main idea
- **Speaking:** talking about past events in your life

Vocabulary focus

- Life events: *start a course, get a job, get married, move to another town*

Review

Ask students to find the sentences they wrote for homework for Unit 4 Lesson 3. Elicit sentences about some (or all) of the people in the class, eg *Has anyone got a sentence about Paolo?*

1

This activity introduces the concept of past experiences and the age at which they happened. Students should not be expected to produce correct forms but may want to try to talk about some of the topics with a partner. The same topics will come up later in the lesson when students will have acquired the language to describe them in more detail.

2

Ask students to cover the texts in Activity 2 and focus on the pictures. Elicit key vocabulary. Then ask students to describe some differences between each pair of pictures,
eg *The boy is inside in one picture. He is looking out of the window.*
Ask students to look at the pictures of Cabinda and Martha as adults (they are shown in the centre, between the pairs of pictures) and establish the fact that they are remembering past events.
Then ask students to read the two narratives silently and choose the best picture for each story.

Answers

Cabinda: *picture 2*
Martha: *picture 4*

These two narratives could then be used to focus on the forms and use of the past simple. Ask students to underline the eight verbs in the first text. Check these (*started, was, stayed, was, saw, looked, saw, took*) and write them on the board in two columns, regular and irregular.
Then elicit how regular past tenses are formed and practise the pronunciation. You could point out here that, although the spelling is the same, there are three ways of pronouncing the *-ed* ending: *started /ɪd/, stayed /d/, looked /t/*. As further regular verbs are introduced during the lesson, you could ask the students which group they belong to.
Explain to the students that many common verbs are irregular and have to be learnt separately. Check that they know the present forms for these verbs.
Stress to the students that the time of these events is known. Check by asking questions, eg:
How old was Cabinda?
When did he go into the classroom?
Is Cabinda a child now?

Ask students to look through the second narrative and underline the past tense verbs. They then add to the lists of regular and irregular verbs.
The final lists for the two texts should look like this:

Regular	Irregular
started /ɪd/	was/were
stayed /d/	saw
looked /t/	took
stopped /t/	went
	came

3

Students now listen to Cabinda talking about more events in his life. Establish that he now does two jobs, teacher and disc jockey. Ask students to read through the table before listening. Check that they know how years are expressed in English, eg 1986 (*nineteen eighty-six*) and practise this if necessary.

▣ Play the cassette once, advising students to listen for the years only.

Play the cassette again for the remaining information. Let students check in pairs and then play the cassette again. Check the answers and write the completed text on the board.

Answers

year	event
1986	He left college.
	He got a *job* as a *TV* journalist.
1988	He *got* engaged but it didn't work out very well.
1989	He moved to another *town*.
	He got a job as a *teacher*, teaching *English*.
1991	He went to *England* to do a *course*.
1992	He went *back* to Mozambique and worked as a *teacher* and *disc jockey*.
1993	He got *married*.

Underline the verbs *left, got, moved*(/d/) *worked*(/t/) and add them to the lists of regular and irregular verbs. You may want to use the table on Practice page 78 Exercise 1 for this.

4

Tell students about two or three important events in your life. Write the date and a sentence on the board for each one, eg
1982 I fell off a horse.
1984 I drove a car for the first time.
1990 I visited England.

Ask students to work in groups and write similar sentences about their own experiences, including accidents, career moves, journeys, relationships, etc. Encourage them to find at least two for each person in the group.

5

The table in this activity could be reproduced as a poster or done on the board. With a large class, it may need to be expanded, eg with more years or more spaces for each year. Ask students to read out sentences about the people in their group. Fill in the table as they speak, correcting any mistakes and discussing past forms. Try to find at least one thing for each year.

The class may have already wanted to find out more about some of these events and asked some further questions. Now focus on the question forms given below the table and practise them by asking more about the events in the table.

If you have time, you could practise question forms further by asking students to write questions to ask Martha and Cabinda about the events described in Activity 2.

Homework

This is a written expansion of the discussion in Activity 5.

Practice *page 78*

1

Refer the students to Lesson 1 Activity 2 and follow the Teacher's notes for the presentation of the forms and use of the past simple tense.
Ask students to complete the table which includes most of the past tense verbs from the lesson.

Answers

look	looked
move	moved
start	started
stay	stayed
stop	stopped
work	worked

come	came
get	got
go	went
have	had
leave	left
see	saw
take	took

2

Language Summary 2 focuses on past time references. Exercise 2 continues the story of Martha's life. Exercises 2 and 3 practise the use of the past simple with time references and past question forms.

Answers

In 1980 Martha started her three-year course at College. In 1983 she *left* College and *got* married. One year later she *went* to Maputo and in 1985 she *had* a baby. The next year she *got* a job as a teacher. In 1991 she *went** to England and then in 1992 she *went* back to Mozambique.

Note *If students are in England, then *came* would be more appropriate here.

3

Answers

2 *When did you get engaged?*
3 *When did you move to Maputo?*
4 *When did you start learning English?*
5 *When did you visit Cambridge?*
6 *When did you leave college?*

Lesson 2 *First job*

Aims: To introduce the language of comparison and give further practice in past simple, introducing negative forms.

Language focus

1 Comparatives:
   (with nouns)
   I'm going to a lot **more parties**.
   (with adverbs)
   I work **more carefully**.
   (adjectives)
   You work **longer hours**.
   You are **more independent**.

2 Past simple negative
   At school I **didn't get up** so early.

Skills focus

- **Reading:** a magazine article for the main idea and detail
- **Speaking:** taking part in a roleplay about jobs

Vocabulary focus

- Working conditions: *hours, travel, holidays, money*
- Travel: *travel agent, trains, flights, prices, dates*

Review

You could ask a few students to read out their stories about an event in the past. With classes of older students some of these may include jobs. This would be a good lead-in to the topic of Lesson 2.

1

Ask students about their experience of school:
Do/did you like school? Why/why not?

Then ask them to do Activity 1 individually and afterwards to compare opinions in pairs. (This is an opinion activity and there are no correct answers.)
Discuss any more differences between school and work.

2

The first part of the reading activity develops scanning skills. Students look quickly through the article to find the answers to the three questions.
Encourage students to do this as quickly as possible. Avoid focusing on vocabulary at this stage.

Answers

1 *travel agent*	2 *in London*	3 *yes*

3

Students now read the text again to identify which topics are mentioned. These topics are related to those in Activity 1.

Answers

- [ ] money
- [✓] hours of work
- [✓] travelling to work
- [✓] meeting people
- [✓] parties
- [ ] holidays

4

This activity focuses on the contrast between present activities (at work) and past activities (at school).

Answers

2 *at work* 3 *at school* 4 *at work* 5 *at work* 6 *at school*

This would be a good time to introduce the past simple negative (see Language Summary 2) and do Practice page 79 Exercise 3.

5

This is the first extended roleplay and needs to be carefully prepared.

First establish the two characters involved (Sheree's schoolfriend and Sheree) and the time of the roleplay (the end of Sheree's first *day* at work), which is different from the time described in the magazine article (the end of her first *year* at work).

Elicit from students what they know about Sheree's first day at work:

What time did she get up?
How did she travel to work?
Where was the office?
What problems did she have on her first day? Why?
How long was her journey home?

Decide which students are A (Sheree's schoolfriend) and which are B (Sheree).

Put small groups of As and Bs together to prepare.

Tell As to prepare correct questions from the prompts given on the rolecard.

Tell Bs to prepare to talk about their first day at work. They should use the information from the magazine article but also invent extra details about their first day at work, using the prompts on the rolecard to help them.

Circulate and help as necessary.

Regroup the students into pairs, A and B. Tell them to begin the conversation as shown in the example.

Monitor and note down any important problems but encourage fluency rather than accuracy at this stage.

The language of comparison could be introduced either at this stage or in a subsequent lesson of its own, using Language Summary 1 and the exercises on Practice page 79.

Homework

This is a written follow-up to the roleplay with an alternative for those students who are already at work.

Practice *page 79*

Language Summary 1

Refer students back to Unit 5 Lesson 2 (page 32) and ask them to find the four examples given at the beginning of Language Summary 1. Then see if they can find further examples of similar constructions on page 32.

Elicit the basic rules for the formation of comparatives.

Although students are meeting comparatives with nouns, adverbs and adjectives, the pattern is similar: **more** is used with everything except short adjectives.

(At this level, the use of the comparative with two-syllable adjectives such as **boring** and with irregular adverbs such as **fast** and **hard** is not explored.)

1

Prepare for Exercise 1 by talking about the two jobs and encouraging students to compare them.

Then students do the exercise. They check it in pairs.

Answers

2 *Sheree works longer hours.*
3 *Rodolfo has longer holidays.(or Rodolfo has more holidays.)*
4 *Sheree goes to more parties.*
5 *Rodolfo's job is more artistic.*
6 *Sheree gets more money.*
7 *Sheree's/Rodolfo's job is easier. (students' choice)*
8 *Sheree's/Rodolfo's job is more interesting. (students' choice)*

2

This exercise gives further practice with adjective comparisons.

Check that students are spelling the comparative forms of short adjectives correctly, eg *easy – easier, big – bigger.*

Answers

2 *safer*
3 *faster*
4 *more comfortable*
5 *easier*
6 *cheaper*

3

Refer students back to Lesson 2 Activity 4.

Elicit full sentences from the prompts and answers, eg
At school she wanted to work in travel.
At school she didn't like maths.

Elicit the formation of the negative with *didn't* and extend to the verb *to be: wasn't/weren't.* Exercise 3 gives practice in both of these.

Answers

2 At school *I didn't work long hours.*
3 At school *I didn't go to a lot of parties.*
4 At school *I wasn't friendly with older people.*
5 At school *I didn't meet the public.*
6 At school *I didn't have money to spend.*

4

This gives further practice in all past tense forms.

Answers

2 Mike *took* his final exam in 1983.
3 Did you *get* married before you came to England?
4 I *played* football when I was a child.
5 Cabinda *stopped* playing football when he had an accident.
6 I *came* back to England in 1993.
7 Did you go to Spain when you *were* a child?

Lesson 3 *Are you old enough?*

Aim: To extend the language of comparison to include superlative forms.

Language focus

1 Superlative forms
   The youngest person in Britain to have a university degree

2 *Should* for expressing opinion
   I think the minimum age to go to university **should** be seventeen.

Skills focus

- **Reading:** a newspaper article for detail
- **Listening:** to a radio news item for detail and listening to a talk for specific information

Vocabulary focus

- Education: *university degree, course, classes, lessons, graduate*
- Activities regulated by age: *ride a moped, buy alcoholic drinks, leave school, buy cigarettes*
- Jobs: *professional footballer, pilot, teacher*
- Ages: *thirteen-year-old, eighteen, 101-year-old, youngest, of his own age, the minimum/maximum age*

Review

Collect in the written homework from Lesson 2. Focus on mistakes with comparative forms and past simple when correcting it.

Warmer

Before the students open their books, write the following words on the board:
   boy   university   thirteen   mathematics   proud

Ask the students to make two sentences including all these words (and adding other necessary words).
Ask for some of the sentences. Then lead on to a presentation of key vocabulary: *genius, degree, qualifications.*

1

As preparation for the reading activity, you could ask students to work in pairs and copy the form from Activity 1. Then ask them to interview each other and complete this form with information from their partner.
Next ask students to read the newspaper article and fill in the form for the boy in the article. Point out that they will not be able to complete the whole form yet.
⬚ Now play the cassette, which gives another version of the same news story. Students can complete the form with the information from the cassette.

Answers

Name:	Ganesh Sittampalam
Address:	Surbiton, South London.
Age:	13
Qualifications:	degree in mathematics
Spare time interests:	television, football

2

Ask students to read the text given in Activity 2 and predict the missing verbs in pairs.
⬚ Play the cassette again so that they can check their predictions.

Answers

1 *became*	**2** *was*	**3** *started*	**4** *went*
5 *did*	**6** *watches*	**7** *plays*	**8** *said*

3

Ask students to work in groups and complete the table with the minimum ages for these activities in their countries.
Make sure that students understand that the word *minimum* means the youngest legal age.
⬚ Then play the cassette and ask the students to fill in the minimum ages for Britain.

Answers

	Your country	Britain
ride a moped		16
ride a motorbike		17
drive a car		17
buy alcoholic drinks		18
buy cigarettes		16
leave school		16
get married (with parents' permission)		16
get married (without parents' permission)		18

4

In this activity, students express their own opinions about minimum and maximum ages for different activities.
You could ask them to work in groups and then compare and see how far they agree.
You may want to present *should* using Practice page 80 Language Summary 2 and do Exercise 3 on the same page as preparation for the discussion in Activity 4.

Homework

Elicit some ideas from the class. Possibilities include: *bungy jumping, skydiving, sailing round the world, writing a best selling book (about ...?), being a pop star.*
Encourage students to follow the same format as in the article about Ganesh.

Practice *page 80*

Language Summary 1

Ask students to think back to Ganesh.
Elicit why he is famous. (*He's **the youngest** person in Britain to have a university degree.*)
Use this to present the superlative, both form and meaning.
The exercises on this page focus on adjective forms.

1

Students could do this exercise in pairs.

Answers

2 *The longest* river
3 *The highest* mountain
4 *The oldest* building
5 *The largest* lake
6 *The most* romantic city

Students' ideas for sentences 7, 8 and 9 could be expanded and used as a quiz for the class, or different classes could write quizzes for each other.

2

Ask students to read the texts in Exercise 2 and complete the table.

Answers

Name	Youngest or oldest?	Record	Age
Ruth Kistler	oldest	mother	57
Jackie Coogan	youngest	millionaire	6
David Cooper	oldest man	passed driving test	89
Gerty Edwards-Land	oldest woman	passed driving test	90

3

Refer students to the model in the speech bubble in Lesson 3 Activity 4, where *should* is used to express an opinion.
Use Exercise 3 for controlled practice of this.

4

This exercise recycles expressions about age from Lesson 3.
You could expand it if your class want to know/have met other expressions, eg *middle-aged, in his teens, in her thirties, elderly.*

Answers

1 *the youngest*
2 *thirteen-year-old*
3 *of his own age*
4 *The oldest*
5 *maximum*

The theme of this unit is relationships, in particular between friends and flatmates. Students learn how to describe how they first met someone. They also talk about personal habits, and how these affect other people.

Lesson 1 *Just good friends*

Aims: To talk and write about the topic of friends and friendship.

Language focus

1 Joining sentences with *and* and *but*
   I have fun with my friends **and** laugh a lot with them.
   I like my brother a lot **but** he's not my best friend.

2 *It* as subject with adjectives
   It's possible for men and women to be friends.

Skills focus

• **Speaking:** exchanging opinions about friendship
• **Writing:** a short poem in a group

Vocabulary focus

• Friendship: *new friends, close friends, best friend, just friends, good friends*
• Communicating: *laugh, tell, argue with, write letters, share feelings, have fun with, listen to problems*

Review

Collect in the articles about 101-year-olds from Unit 5 Lesson 3, correct them and then display them as a wall newspaper.

Warmer

With students' books closed, write the letters *I N D E F R* on the board and tell the students to make a word. (*FRIEND*).
Ask students how many words they can think of to describe friends, eg *good* friends.
Make a list of correct suggestions on the board.

1

Ask students to look through the sentences in Activity 1 and see how many of the suggestions from the Warmer they can find.
Check understanding of the sentences, eg *argue with/laugh*.

Then do Activity 1 as follows:
1 Students work alone to complete column 1.
2 Students interview partners to complete column 2.
🔲 3 Students listen to the cassette and complete the column for Phil.
🔲 4 Students listen again and complete the column for Helen.
Ask the class if there are any sentences which have ticks in all four columns.

Answers

	Phil	Helen
2	x	✓
3	✓	✓
4	x	x
5	x	✓
6	x	✓
7	✓	x

2

Before the students start, elicit the difference in use between *and* and *but*. You could do Practice page 81, Exercise 1 here.
Then ask them to do the activity and check the answers with a partner.

Answers

   2 *f*
   3 *c*
   4 *b*
   5 *a*
   6 *d*

Ask the class which sentences they agree with.
Practice page 81, Exercise 2 gives more practice in using *and* and *but* and would fit in well here.

3

Write the examples on the board and elicit one or two more ideas from the class. Then ask students to continue the list in pairs.
Ask each pair to join another pair, pool their ideas and finally produce a list of five qualities in order of importance.

4

For this activity you need at least four strips of paper for each student, glue and large sheets of paper for the poems.
Put the students in groups of about six. Make sure these groups are different from the last activity.
Ask the class to write a sentence beginning *A friend is ...* on their first strip of paper. Students should not talk or compare sentences at this stage.
Then repeat this procedure with the second, third and fourth strips of paper.
Each time the students begin *A friend is ...* and write a different definition.

Then ask students to look at all the sentences for their group together, make any necessary corrections together and choose the best eight sentences to make a poem.
They can stick these on the large sheets of paper in the order they want and decorate the paper, choose a title and then display or read out their poems to the class.

Homework

Go through the questions quickly with the class when setting the homework.

Practice *page 81*

1

Refer students to Lesson 1 Activity 2 and to Language Summary 1. Exercise 1 practises *and* and *but* using the context of Phil and his friends.

Answers

  2 *and*   3 *but*   4 *and*   5 *but*

2

Exercise 2 extends the use of *and* and *but* to other contexts.

Answers

  2 That car is very fast *but it's not very comfortable.*
  3 You can learn English at that school *but you can't learn German.*
  4 He's got dark hair *and his eyes are dark too.*
  5 In the town you can go shopping *but the shops are very expensive.*
  6 She works long hours *but she gets a lot of money.*
  7 At the sports centre there's a basketball court *but there isn't a swimming pool.*

3

This language point occurs in sentence 7 of Activity 1 and covers the 'dummy' use of *it* to refer to something defined later in the sentence.
Exercise 3 practises the common pattern *It is ... (for someone) to ....* Note that an adjective fills the first space and a verb phrase the second.

Answers

  2 *It is lovely to see you again.*
  3 *It is easy for children to learn languages.*
  4 *It is important for a pilot to speak English.*
  5 *It is impossible to live without water.*
  6 *It is expensive for a family to go skiing in Italy.*

4

This recycles and extends the collocations from the Warmer in Lesson 1.

Answers

  1 a *good* friend
  2 a *close* friend
  3 a *new* friend
  4 a *best* friend
  5 *old*
  6 *school*
  7 *boy*
  8 *girl*

Lesson 2 *How did you meet?*

Aims: To give practice in describing sequences of events in the past and in following instructions.

Language focus

1 Imperatives
   Write the name of a famous man.
   Fold the paper over.

2 Sequencers
   First, take a sheet of paper.
   Finally, write 'The result was ...'
   When I got home, I decided to give Gary a call.

Skills focus

- **Reading:** narratives for the main ideas and inferring meaning
- **Writing:** a narrative in the first person

Vocabulary focus

- Relationships: *family, boyfriend, go out with, become friends, get to know, get on well*
- Colloquial language: *brilliant, great, for ages*
- Verbs for instructions: *fold, write, pass on, repeat, take*

Review

For homework the students should have written a description of one of their friends. This could be used to link the last lesson with this one. Students could choose a partner and exchange papers with them, or volunteers could read part or all of their descriptions aloud.

Warmer

Ask a few students when/how they met the friend they described for homework. Keep this brief as students talk about it in more detail in Activity 4.

1

Ask students to read the four stories in Activity 1 and underline the names of the four men mentioned.
Look at the photograph of the first man and ask the students how they know it is John. Elicit reasons, eg he's old and we know they met thirty years ago.
Then ask them to use the information in the other stories to match the names to the other men in the photographs.

Answers

> John – given as example – **Text 3**
> Paul – man with tennis racquet – **Text 1**
> Gary – boy with phone – **Text 4**
> Jim – boy in school uniform – **Text 2**

2

This activity develops more intensive reading skills. Questions 6 and 7 also involve some inference.

Answers

2 *Jim*	**3** *John/Paul*	**4** *Jim*
5 *Paul*	**6** *Gary*	**7** *John*

3

In this activity students need to think about the main idea of each story. They should be encouraged to be creative with the title for Text 2. Tell students to keep the title short.

Answers

> Friends for life – *Text 3*
> The boy next door – *Text 1*
> Ideas for Text 2 – *School Romance, Love in the Laboratory, Lesson of Love*

4

Give students a little time to prepare their answers before they start talking. As an example you could talk about how you met a friend.

5

Students may already know this game, which is called 'Consequences' in English.
▱ Give students time to read through the instructions before they listen. Then play the cassette.
Help students with vocabulary before they start the game.

Answers

2 *c*	**3** *b*	**4** *g*
5 *e*	**6** *a*	**7** *d*

6

Put the students into groups to play the game.
Either let each group work at its own pace with group leaders reading out the instructions or read out the instructions yourself to all the groups simultaneously.
Ask each group to read their best story out to the class.

Homework

Students have a choice of homework. The first option is more controlled but needs careful introduction by the teacher, with reference to the example. You could finish the example story with the class and then ask them to choose a different one for homework.
The second option is less controlled and is a written version of Activity 4. It could be seen as a second part to the homework from Unit 6 Lesson 1.

Practice *page 82*

Language Summary 1

Refer students back to the instructions for the game in Lesson 2 Activity 5. Ask them to underline the verbs which told them what to do, eg *repeat*, *write*, *pass*, etc.
Use Language Summary 1 to explain the form and use of the imperative.

1

Ask students to do Exercise 1. Help with vocabulary as necessary.

Answers

2 Put your card in the slot.
3 Dial the number you want.
4 When you've finished talking, replace the handset.
5 Take your card out of the machine.

2

This activity practises the negative form of the imperative. Ask students to read through the instructions and suggest where they might see similar instructions. Then ask them to write the opposite instructions.

Answers

2 *OPEN THIS SIDE*
3 *DO NOT FOLD HERE*
4 *DO NOT BREAK GLASS*
5 *PLEASE PHONE AFTER 5.00 PM*
6 *PLEASE DO NOT PARK HERE*
7 *WRITE YOUR NAME HERE*

Language Summary 2

Look at Language Summary 2 with the students and ask them to find some examples of sequencers in Lesson 2 page 38 (*after*, *when*).

3

Then ask them to order the story in Exercise 3.

Answers

2 I first met her when I was in Istanbul on business ...
3 When I went back to America I gave her my phone number.
4 Soon afterwards she came to New York on business ...
5 After that we didn't see one another for ...
6 Then I went back to Istanbul ...
7 Finally we decided not to see one another again.

4

This practises the more colloquial expressions from the lesson.

Answers

2 *to go out together*
3 *to get to know someone*
4 *to give someone a call*
5 *to have a brilliant time*
6 *to keep in touch*

Lesson 3 *Living alone, living together*

Aims: To talk about similarities and differences between people and the problems this can cause when they share accommodation.

Language focus

1 Similarities and differences
  I smoke. **So do I/I don't.**
  I'm tidy. **So am I/I'm not.**

2 Could for possibility
  Nick **could** share a flat with Takashi.

Skills focus

- **Listening:** for detail to two people talking about sharing accommodation
- **Speaking:** taking part in a discussion to solve a problem

Vocabulary focus

- Personal habits and preferences: *to smoke, to get up early/late, to like parties/loud music*
- Personal qualities: *tidy, vegetarian, talkative, sociable*
- Jobs: *singer, bass guitarist, trainee manager, designer, air hostess*

Review

Students who chose the first homework option from Unit 6 Lesson 2 could read their stories out to the class. Or you could revise the vocabulary of relationships and colloquial language from the last lesson.

Warmer

Find out if any students have shared a room with a brother or sister or have lived alone. Did they like it? Were there any problems?

1

Look at the vocabulary in Activity 1 with the students and then ask them to tick the statements that are true for them. Before they compare answers in pairs or groups, teach the expressions in the speech bubbles, drilling the language as necessary. Make sure the students understand the use of the different auxiliary verbs.
Elicit students' opinions on which differences can cause problems when sharing accommodation.

2

🔲 This activity reinforces the vocabulary from Activity 1. Students may be able to get the information the first time they listen.

Answers

1 *Their bedrooms were untidy.*
2 *They're both vegetarian.*

3

🔲 Ask the students to listen the first time to find out if Bruce was happy about sharing with his friend or not.
Then give time for them to read through the text and see if they can fill in any gaps. Finally play the cassette again.

Answers

2 *untidy*
3 *tidy*
4 *visitors*
5 *friends*
6 *earlier*
7 *played*
8 *like*

4

Pre-teach the jobs vocabulary. Then ask the students to read the information and work with a partner to solve the flat-sharing problems.

When reporting back, students should give reasons, which might lead to a short discussion.

Answers

(This is fairly open-ended and alternative answers are possible.)

2 *Takashi (because of the dog) or*
Leslie (he likes parties, she is quiet; he gets up late)

3 *Takashi, Nick and Christine (all quiet)*
or Alex, Amira and Leslie (Alex is out in the evening, Amira and Leslie are both sociable. Although Amira doesn't smoke and Leslie does.)

Practice page 83 Language Summary 2 and Exercise 3 would fit in well here.

Homework

Prepare for this by extending the discussion in Activity 4, getting the students to give their own views. Remind them that they have to write full sentences about the people (the information is given in note form).

Practice *page 83*

1

Refer students back to Lesson 3 Activity 1.
Revise the language for expressing similarities and differences, using Language Summary 1.
In Exercise 1 students have to recognize the correct forms.

Answers

2 *b*
3 *e*
4 *f*
5 *a*
6 *d*
7 *c*

2

In Exercise 2 students produce the language themselves.
No set answers as answers depend on students.

3

Students met this language in Lesson 3 Activity 4. Use the Language Summary to teach *could* for possibility. Then ask students to do Exercise 3.

Answers

2 *could*
3 *couldn't*
4 *could*
5 *couldn't*
6 *couldn't*
7 *couldn't*

4

Remind students about word stress, using the examples in Exercise 4. Ask the students to try grouping the words. Then read them aloud for them to check/finish the exercise.

■ ■ ■	■ ■ ■
manager	guitarist
sociable	instructions
talkative	important
travelling	together
visitors	

The theme of this unit is leaving the place where you live – either your house or your country – and the challenge of adapting to a new lifestyle, including language and money problems.

Lesson 1 *Leaving home*

Aim: To compare past and present lifestyles for someone who has left home.

Language focus

1 Revision of present simple and past simple (and comparison of their forms)
He **shares** the flat with his brother.
Roy **moved** into a flat four years ago.
2 Expressions of time
Roy moved into a flat **four years ago**.
The worst thing about living in a flat is the cold **in winter**.

Skills focus

- **Reading:** a magazine article for detail and looking at text organization
- **Writing:** notes and messages

Vocabulary focus

- Homes and household equipment: *a 3-bedroomed flat, kitchen, bathroom, electric heaters, front door, kitchen table, washing machine*
- Household activities: *washing, ironing, do the housework, pay the telephone bill*

Review

As feedback from the homework in Unit 6 Lesson 3, ask students to report back in groups who they could/couldn't share flats with from the six people described in Activity 4. Ask groups to find out who are the most popular/least popular people to share with.

Warmer

In preparation for the lesson, write some or all of the words from the Vocabulary focus above on the board in jumbled order and ask students to categorize them into three groups: *Places in the house, Equipment in the house, Activities in the house.*

1

Ask students to look at the picture of Roy and, in pairs, list three possible reasons why he is leaving home.
▭ Play the first part of the cassette to see if anyone guessed exactly why he is leaving.
Play the complete section and ask students to fill in the chart.

Answers

Age when he left	Why he left	Where he went to live
Roy 20	*to be independent*	*in a flat*
David 22	*problems with dad*	*in a flat with Roy*

Practice page 84 Exercise 2 is a completion exercise based on the script of this recording and could be done here.

2

Ask students to look at the text and tell you how many paragraphs there are. (*four*)
Then ask them to find the main topic of each paragraph as quickly as they can.

Answers

1 What Roy thinks about living in a flat.
2 Who he lives with.
3 The main problem with living in a flat.
4 The good things about living in a flat.

3

This activity requires more detailed reading.

Answers

2 false
3 true
4 true
5 false
6 false
7 false

4

Before Activity 4, you could look at Practice page 84 Language Summary 2, which gives information about expressions of time. Or this could be used to follow up if students have problems with this activity.

Answers

2 Roy's flat is cold in winter.
3 Roy did not do his own washing and ironing when he lived with his mum and dad.
4 Roy often spends all his money before the end of the week.
5 He doesn't get bored on Thursday nights.

Practice page 84 Exercise 3 gives practice in using similar expressions to describe students' own experience.

5

Introduce the idea of leaving messages for flatmates and elicit why Roy and David often had to do this. (Because they worked at different times and didn't see each other very often.) Ask students to match the messages with the places.

Answers

> **2** *on the kitchen table*
> **3** *on the front door*
> **4** *by the telephone*
> **5** *on the washing machine*
> **6** *in a local newspaper*

Homework

Encourage students to use the models in Activity 5. You may want to do the first message together as a class.

Practice *page 84*

Language Summary 1

Ask students what they remember about Roy's past and his present situation. Then focus on the verb forms used and refer to Language Summary 1 to look at the differences in meaning between the present simple and the past simple.

1

Exercise 1 focuses on the forms of the two tenses and emphasizes their similarities.

Answers

PRESENT SIMPLE	PAST SIMPLE
Affirmative	**Affirmative**
He *lives* in a flat.	He *lived* in a flat.
Question	**Question**
Does he *live* in a flat?	*Did* he *live* in a flat?
Negative	**Negative**
He *doesn't live* in a house.	He *didn't live* in a house.
Question tags	**Question tags**
He lives in a flat, *doesn't* he?	He lived in a flat, *didn't* he?
He doesn't live at home, *does* he?	He didn't live at home, *did* he?
Short answers	**Short answers**
Yes, he *does*.	Yes, he *did*.
No, he *doesn't*.	No, he *didn't*.

2

As this is the tapescript for Unit 7 Lesson 1 Activity 1, students could complete it and then listen to the cassette again to check their answers.

Answers

> **2** *moved*
> **3** *did* you *leave*
> **4** *wanted*
> **5** *like*
> **6** *did* he *leave*
> **7** *had*
> **8** *left*
> **9** *Do* you often *go*
> **10** *go*

3

Refer back to Lesson 1 Activity 4.
Elicit or present the expressions of time given in Language Summary 2.
Ask students to complete Exercise 3 with information about themselves. Circulate and monitor.

Answers

> **2** *When* I was a child I lived ...
> **3** Five years *ago* I ...
> **4** *In* winter I like ...
> **5** *In* the evenings I go ...
> **6** *At* night when I don't go out, I like ...
> **7** Two days *ago*, I went ...
> **8** *At* nine o'clock tonight, I want to ...

Lesson 2 *In another country*

Aims: To introduce the language of travel and tourism and to practise the language of common situations when visiting another country.

Language focus

Can and *could* for ability
How many languages **can** you speak?
Jacky **couldn't** read Arabic.

Skills focus

- **Listening:** identifying the main topics in a talk and listening for detail
- **Reading:** a fax which asks for information
- **Writing:** giving information about your region/country

Vocabulary focus

- Countries and languages: *England, Sudan, Arabic, Japanese, Greek, Russian, English*
  Jacky comes from **England**.
  She speaks **English**.
- Communication: *speak, write, read, signs, talk, phrase book, fax, alphabet*
- Places for tourists: *hotel, restaurant, market, garage, airport, station*
- Things tourists need: *breakfast, bathroom, a table for three, a non-smoking seat, souvenirs*

Review

Ask students to compare in pairs the messages they wrote for homework. Elicit suggestions and write model answers on the board.

1

Ask students to make a list of the countries they have visited and ask them about the languages they can speak/read. Then explain Activity 1 and tell them to work in pairs to find the solution. This is possible even if they don't know any of the languages.

Answers

> **1 and 7** *Arabic*
> **2 and 5** *Japanese*
> **3 and 6** *Russian*
> **4 and 8** *Greek*
>
> **TAXI**   3   5   8
> **WAY OUT**   4   6   7

Ask students if they know any of these languages. If students are having problems with country names and languages, you could look at Practice page 85, Exercise 3 and the related vocabulary section.

2

Ask students to read the questions so that they know what they are listening for.
 Play the cassette, twice if necessary.

Answers

> 1 *Sudan*   2 *Arabic*   3 *No*   4 *No*

3

Encourage students to guess the meaning of *market* and *mechanic*. Then tell them to choose, in pairs, two situations where Jacky could manage to communicate in English and two where she might have difficulty.
Ideas: Do taxi drivers usually speak English? Could you point to what you want in some situations?
 Now play the cassette for the students to compare with their predictions.

Answers

> ☒ in taxis   ☒ in the market
> ☑ in restaurants   ☑ talking to a mechanic

4

Encourage students to think first about how a phrase book is organised and how it is different from a dictionary.
Then ask them to match the sections with the questions that follow.

Answers

1 *f, a*
2 *g, i*
3 *c, e*
4 *d, j*
5 *b, h*

This activity could be extended in monolingual classes by asking students to prepare a phrase book for an English person coming to their country. Different groups could do different sections, giving English phrases and their translations, and then students could compare and comment on each other's. Multilingual classes could work out an English phrase book (without translations), using the sections in Activity 4 and other sections if they wanted to, eg in a language school.

5

This could be done as a whole class if the students are all from the same region, otherwise in groups, pairs or individually. Students could make notes in preparation for the homework.

Homework

This relates to Activity 5 but students can add more information if they want to.

Practice *page 85*

Language Summary

Refer students back to Lesson 2 Activity 1 and the question
*'How many languages **can** you speak?'*
Explain that here **can** is used for ability.
Give further examples, eg
*I **can** ride a bicycle*
*I **can** swim*
Elicit the past and the negative forms.

1

Exercise 1 could be practised orally first, and then written.

Answers

2 *Jacky couldn't use a computer but David can.*
3 *Jacky couldn't use a video but David can.*
4 *Jacky could tell the time but David can't.*
5 *Jacky could swim but David can't.*
6 *Jacky couldn't count to ten in French but David can.*

2

This is a less controlled activity, where students are writing about themselves.

3

The list of countries and languages can be expanded according to the students' knowledge and interest. Encourage students to identify the typical endings for language names, eg *-ish, -an, -ese*, and to note changes in stress patterns.

Answers

Country	Language
■ ■ England	■ ■ English
■ Spain	■ ▪ Spanish
■ ■ Turkey	■ ■ Turkish
■ ■ ■ Italy	■ ■ ■ Italian
■ ■ Russia	■ ■ Russian
■ ■ ■ Germany	■ ■ German
▪ ■ Japan	■ ■ ■ Japanese
■ ■ China	■ ■ Chinese
■ ■ ▪ Portugal	■ ■ ■ Portuguese

Lesson 3 *Let the kids pay the bills*

Aim: To find out about a major change in a family's life-style.

Language focus

1 Subject and object pronouns and possessive adjectives
   You use this house like a hotel.
   I was sick of doing everything for **them**.
   Andrea and Nigel lived with **their** son and daughter.

2 *Must* for necessity.
   I **must** pay the electricity bill today.

Skills focus

- **Reading:** a newspaper article for the main ideas and detail
- **Speaking:** roleplaying a phone conversation between members of a family
- **Listening:** for specific information and detail

Vocabulary focus

- Colloquial **language:** *to have enough, to be sick of, kids*
- More household **activities:** *pay the bills, electricity bill, keep the house clean, pay the rent, rent out a room*
- More family members: *children, kids, parents, son, daughter*

Review

With a monolingual class, students could compare their homework (from Unit 7 Lesson 2) to see if they have recommended the same places and to check language. With a multilingual class, students could exchange the letters in order to find out about each other's regions.

Warmer

Brainstorm differences between living in a house and staying in a hotel, eg house – *you probably cook your own food; hotel – you don't make your own bed.*

1

Tell the students this lesson is about a family who change the way they live. Ask them to do Activity 1, discussing in pairs and writing *parents* or *children* beside each speech bubble. This activity leads in to the reading text as students have thought about what normally happens and then read about a different situation in the text.

2

Before answering the questions in Activity 2, ask the students to scan the text to find the names of the four people in the article and their relationship to one another.
Draw a family tree on the board.
Then ask students to read and answer the two questions in Activity 2.

Answers

1 *Mark and Sally (the 'kids')*
2 *Andrea and Nigel (the parents)*

3

Activity 3 demands closer reading and some inference skills.

Answers

1 *Andrea had to do everything for the children, and four people in one small house was too much for them.*
2 *For Nigel and Andrea to leave home.*

4

Students now hear Nigel telling the rest of the story on the cassette. Ask them to read the questions through before listening, and to write short answers.

Answers

1 *No.*
2 *OK.*
3 *They both have jobs.*
4 *Nigel and Andrea's old bedroom.*
5 *In the country.*
6 *Smaller (just big enough for two).*
7 *In a bookshop.*
8 *Nigel and Andrea.*

The tapescript is also used as a text for the completion exercise on Practice page 86 (Exercise 3), which focuses on pronoun use. You could use this at this point, but it does demand some preparatory work on pronouns and possessive adjectives. (See Language Summary 1.)

5

This is similar to the roleplay in Unit 5 Lesson 2 'First job' in that it is based on the text but students need to add extra information and ideas of their own.

The roleplay is done in pairs with one student choosing to be either Nigel or Andrea and the other choosing to be either Mark or Sally.

Students who have chosen the same roles could prepare together. Circulate during the preparation and help with ideas for more questions.

During the roleplay note down the expressions the students are using to say things are alright or not alright. This could then be a language area to focus on. Examples:
Fine! Great! Lovely! Really well!
OK. Alright.
We've got a few problems. It's awful. We're really missing you!

Homework

Brainstorm the types of problems Mark and Sally might have, eg *their friend isn't paying the rent; the dog is sick; the washing machine is broken.*

Students can choose one of these for the homework or make up another.

Practice *page 86*

Language Summary 1

Write the example sentences from Language Summary 1 on the board and underline the pronouns and possessive adjectives. Briefly explain the difference between them

1

Ask the students to complete the table in Exercise 1 in pairs. Then check it carefully before doing Exercises 2 and 3.

Answers

Subject pronoun	Object pronoun	Possessive adjective
I	*me*	my
You	you	*your*
He	*him*	his
She	her	her
It	*it*	its
We	us	*our*
They	them	their

2

You could do this as a competition individually or in groups – over 30 sentences are in fact possible. Before starting, make sure students understand the instructions – they cannot add any extra words but they can use the words in the box as many times as they want.

Examples of possible answers are:
He liked their children.
Children liked it.
They liked her.
Their children liked her children.

3

 This text is the tapescript from Lesson 3 Activity 4, so students could listen to the cassette again to check their answers.

Answers

2 *us*	3 *you*	4 *I*	5 *it*	6 *I*
7 *my*	8 *we*	9 *our*	10 *it*	11 *they*
12 *They*	13 *they*	14 *their*	15 *They*	16 *them*
17 *you*	18 *We*	19 *us*	20 *I*	21 *We*

4

Present *must* for necessity, using the examples in Language Summary 2. Ask students to do Exercise 4 which continues the story of Nigel and Andrea's family.

Answers

2 *mustn't*   3 *must*   4 *must*   5 *mustn't*   6 *must*

This could be extended into another context by asking students in groups to write rules for the classroom.

The theme of this unit is possible life goals and directions. It covers possible changes in individual lifestyles and in the world as a whole. The idea of predicting and planning for the future is introduced.

Lesson 1 *Before I'm old*

Aims: To introduce and practise the language needed to make predictions and talk about possible future events.

Language focus

1 Future with *will* and *might* for prediction
  I think I'**ll** fall in love.
  I **might** start my own business.
  I **don't think I'll** win a lottery.

2 Giving reasons using *because*
  We'll take a gun **because** we might have to kill things.

Skills focus

• **Listening:** to an interview to complete a table
• **Speaking:** making decisions and giving reasons

Vocabulary focus

• Life events: *buy a house, have a lot of children, start your own business, win a lottery,* etc
• The physical world: *planet, weather, seeds, solar panel, diamonds, water*
• Global issues: *world war, politics, government*
• Objects: *gun, knife, pen and paper, money, dictionary*

Review

Before taking in the homework from Unit 7 Lesson 3, you could focus on the format of informal letters and ask students to check that they have followed the conventions, eg how to begin (*Dear mum and dad*), and how to end (*Love from Mark/Sally*). You could ask them to check their own work for correct use of pronouns and possessive adjectives. Then take the homework in for marking.

1

Students could do this in pairs. They will end up with the title of the lesson in the vertical column.

Answers

```
        L I V E  to be 100
      W I N  a lottery
        S T A R T  your own business
          H A V E  a lot of children
      M A K E  a lot of money
            F A L L  in love
          B U Y  a house
      V I S I T  another planet
        S T U D Y  English for a long time
          T R A V E L  to other countries
  R E P R E S E N T  your country in a sport
```

Use the pictures to help explain vocabulary.

2

Make sure the students understand the difference between '*Things I think I'll do*' and '*Things I might do*'. Then ask students to do this individually, by writing 1, 2 or 3 against each line in Activity 1.
After students have compared their answers with a partner, you could find out how far the class agree.

3

This activity extends the theme to more global issues.
You need to look through the table with students first to help with vocabulary and check that they understand the task.
▭ Play the cassette as often as necessary.

Answers

	Probable	Possible	Unlikely
2 There will be big changes in the world's weather.	☐	✔	☐
3 People will live on other planets.	☐	☐	✔
4 There will be one government for the world.	☐	☐	✔
5 There will be another world war.	☐	✔	☐
6 People will live longer.	✔	☐	☐

Then ask students to repeat the interview with a partner, giving their own opinions on these issues. This will prepare them for the next activity.

4

In this activity, students choose the objects according to their own vision of the future. However they must then reach a consensus in their groups and justify their choices. Remind them that they must record their decisions and that they have to think of an extra object to take.

5

Regroup the students to work in pairs with someone from another group.

Homework

This is a written consolidation of Activity 2 but students can also add their own ideas. You could brainstorm some ideas in class if you think your students need help.

Practice *page 87*

Language Summary 1

Refer the students back to Lesson 1 Activity 2.
Focus on the use of *will* and *might* for prediction, using Language Summary 1.

1

Then remind students of the interview with Mike in Lesson 1 Activity 4. Tell them that the table in Exercise 1 shows the results of a similar interview with Mario.

Answers

2 *Mario thinks there will be big changes in the world's weather.*
3 *Mario thinks people might live on other planets.*
4 *Mario thinks there will be one government for the world.*
5 *Mario doesn't think there will be another world war.*
6 *Mario doesn't think people will live for longer.*

2

In this exercise, students make predictions about their own lives in the coming year.

3

Refer students back to Lesson 1 Activity 4, where they gave reasons for their choice of objects.
Focus on *because* and compare it with *and* and *but*. Tell the students that *because* answers the question *Why?*

Answers

2 I might get a new job *and* move to another house.
3 I don't think I'll start a new job *because* I want to continue studying.
4 I don't think I'll win a lottery, *but* I might!
5 I don't think I'll buy a new car *because* they're so expensive.
6 I think in the future people will be healthier *and* they'll live longer.
7 I might fall in love *but* I don't think I'll get married for a long time.

4

In this exercise the students have to mark *only* the main stressed syllable in each word.
Note *Business* is usually pronounced with two syllables only /bɪznɪs/, and *dictionary* with three /dɪk ʃ nrɪ/.

Answers

▪ ■ ▪	■ ▪ ▪
expensive	dictionary
unlikely	government
	politics
	possible
	probable

Lesson 2 *See the world*

Aim: To find out about a student who travelled round Australia between school and university in order to see another part of the world and experience a different lifestyle.

Language focus

1 Relative clauses with *where*
We drove to Brisbane, **where** we got jobs in another restaurant.

2 Time sequencers
First we flew to Sydney.
...then we bought an old car...
After that, we went up to Cairns.
Next we drove across the north of Australia to Darwin.
Finally I returned to Sydney.

Skills focus

- **Reading:** an account of a journey
- **Speaking:** roleplaying a radio interview
- **Listening:** to a radio interview for the main points

Vocabulary focus

- Ways of travelling: *drive, go by air, fly, get a lift, take the bus*
- Expressions of time: *for nine weeks, after a few days, for the next couple of months, just in time for Christmas*
- Direction and location: *in the south-east, up north, near the barrier reef, around the desert, right down south*

Review

Elicit some of the students' predictions from their homework (Unit 8 Lesson 1) and find out how many people think they will travel to different countries in the future.

Warmer

Discuss the countries students would like to travel to. Encourage them to give reasons.

1

Tell the students the lesson is about an English girl who decided to go to Australia.
 Give them time to read through the statements in Activity 1 before playing the cassette.

Answers

2 *false (a pizza restaurant)*
3 *true*
4 *false (for nine months)*
5 *false (Louise)*
6 *false (she wanted to travel)*

2

In this activity the students make short sentences about Alison's journey. The purpose of this is not to predict the exact sentences or phrases that will come in the text but to prepare the students to cope with the longer sentences that they will find in Activity 3.

Possible answers

I/we drove a thousand miles/for a week/across the north of the country.
I drove/went off on my own.
I/we stayed in Sydney/at the next place/for a week.
I/we went to Australia/a thousand miles/across the north of the country.

3

First, students scan for the cities. This should be done very quickly.

Answers

Sydney Brisbane Cairns Darwin Adelaide Melbourne

4

Now students read the passage again to follow the route of Alison's journey and mark it on the map. You may need to tell students where Melbourne is if students find the activity difficult.

Answers

The map could then be used for oral practice and as the basis for further questions about the text.

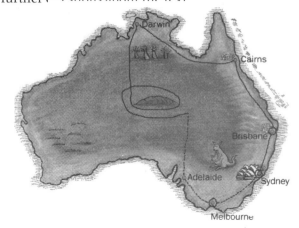

5

Give students time to prepare their roles in groups of As and Bs. Encourage As to make a list of questions to ask and encourage Bs to read the text again to get the details clear in their minds.

Regroup the students into A/B pairs. They can refer to the map but not to the reading text during the roleplay.

You could ask one or two pairs to perform the roleplay in front of the class.

This activity could be extended to interviews about real journeys students in the class have made.

Homework

Students wrote a postcard in Unit 2 Lesson 2 'Dream hotel', but will need reminding of the format and the type of language usually included. Point out the information they should include in the postcard.

Ask the students to try to think of English names and addresses, or give suggestions if necessary.

Practice *page 88*

Language Summary 1

Refer students back to the text in Lesson 2 Activity 3. Ask them to find four examples of relative clauses with *where*. Use Language Summary 1 to explain why and how they are used.

1

Both Exercise 1 and 2 are highly controlled as students would not really be expected to produce this structure at this stage.

Answers

2 *We flew to London, where we stayed for a week in a hotel near Piccadilly Circus.*
3 *He spent the weekend in Athens, where he visited the Acropolis.*
4 *They went to Copacabana beach, where they relaxed in the sun.*
5 *She took her daughter to Florida, where they spent two days at Disneyworld.*
6 *He went on a business trip to Turkey, where his company had their office.*

2

Answers

2 You can go to the Sports Centre, *where you can play volleyball and do aerobics.*
3 You can go shopping in the old town, *where you can buy presents for your friends.*
4 You can take a bus to the beach, *where you can lie in the sun and swim.*
5 You can go to a restaurant, *where you can eat very good seafood.*
6 You can go to the old port, *where you can buy fish from the fishermen.*

3

This is a review and extension of Unit 6 Lesson 2 Language Summary 2. Exercise 3 is productive rather than just receptive. It also gives further practice in describing a journey. Encourage students to use a variety of time sequencers.

Answers

2 Then/next/after that *I went to Rome and stayed for ten days.*
3 Then/next/after that *I went to Venice, but it was very expensive.*
4 When/after I left Venice, *I went to Vienna, where I met Louise.*
5 Then/next/after that *we went to Munich.*
6 When/after I left Munich, *I decided to return to Paris on my own.*
7 Finally *I got back to London and slept for two days!*

Lesson 3 *Time for a change*

Aims: To introduce *going to* to talk about future plans and to continue the theme of changes in lifestyle.

Language focus

1 Future with *going to*
  Mark **is going** to be a journalist.
  Susan **isn't going** to stay at home any more.

2 *somewhere, something, someone*
  She's going to fly **somewhere** hot and sunny.
  Mario is going to do **something** dangerous.
  Someone new is going to join our class next week.

Skills focus

- **Listening:** to people talking about their future plans
- **Writing:** about future plans in a controlled framework
- **Reading:** to identify a sequence of events

Vocabulary focus

- Work: *office, advertisement, ten-month course, journalist, farm, pick fruit*
- Holidays: *five-star hotels, cocktails, sunshine, discos*

Review

Display the postcards the students wrote for their homework around the walls.
Review the content of the last lesson, asking about what Alison did before she went to Australia *(she was at school)*, what she did in Australia *(travelled and got temporary jobs)*, and what she did after the trip *(went to university)*.

Warmer

Ask students about any temporary/holiday jobs they have done. Elicit why they did them and whether they enjoyed them or not.

1

This activity introduces the vocabulary that comes in the lesson.

2

This reading text introduces the context for the first part of the lesson. It gives the students information about Mark's past and some of his future plans. Students have to focus on the sequence of events.

Answers

2 Mark worked in an office.
3 Mark saw an advertisement for a course.
4 Mark decided to change his job.
5 Mark did a ten-month course in journalism.
6 Mark is going to be a journalist.

3

The listening activity gives more details about Mark's plans for the summer now that he is not starting work until October. Play the cassette once for students to answer the first question. The remaining sentences focus on details and give examples of the structure *going to*.

Answers

He's going to work

2 *work*
3 *fruit*
4 *three months*
5 *by train*

Practice page 89 Exercise 1, together with a presentation of *going to*, would fit in well here.

4

Use the picture of Mark's aunt, Susan, to set the context. Ask the questions in Activity 4.

Ask students to decide in pairs what they think Susan is planning to do in the future.

Then play the cassette for students to check their guesses. Then ask them to fill in the gaps and play the cassette once more to check answers.

Answers

> She's 70 this year.
> She's not going to *stay at home* any more.
> She's not going to *listen to the radio* any more.
> She's not going to *clean the house* any more.
> It's time for a change.
> She's going to *get a plane to the sunshine.*
> She's going to *stay in a five-star hotel.*
> She's going to *spend all her money on cocktails and discos.*
> She's going to have the time of her life.
> This year!

Note The tapescript is a little longer than the printed poem.

5

Encourage students to use their own ideas as well as the ideas from this lesson. Circulate and help as necessary.

Ask the students to read out their texts in groups to compare them.

6

This should be done as a class activity. Encourage students to move around and talk to different people. Tell them they can only ask one question to any one person.

When everyone has completed the task, ask the class which names they have for each sentence. Check with the named people that it is true.

Homework

The homework gives intensive written practice of the structure *going to*, focusing on plans for the next week.

Practice *page 89*

Language Summary 1

Refer the students to Lesson 3 Activity 3 and elicit the formation and use of *going to* for future intention.

1

Exercise 1 is related to the topic of the first part of Lesson 3 and gives the students practice in writing sentences with *going to*.

Answers

2 He's *going to pick* fruit.
3 He's *going to sleep in a* tent.
4 He's *going to learn some* Italian.
5 He's *going to earn* a lot of money.
6 He's *going to arrive* on the 21st.
7 *Pete is going to meet him* at the station.

2

Exercise 2 extends the story of Susan's holiday plans. Students write complete sentences, using the pictures as prompts. You may want to do this exercise orally first.

Answers

2 *She's going to buy some suntan lotion/sunbathe.*
3 *She's going to drink cocktails in the sunshine.*
4 *She's going to spend lots of money on clothes.*
5 *She's going to eat in expensive restaurants.*
6 *She's going to go water-skiing.*

Language Summary 2

Ask students where Susan wants to fly to (*somewhere hot and sunny*) and ask them to suggest other words beginning with *some-*. Focus on the examples in Language Summary 2.

3

Then tell students to do Exercise 3, which is about what Mark is going to do for his first job with the newspaper.

Answers

2 *somewhere*
3 *somewhere*
4 *someone*
5 *something*
6 *someone*

This idea could be extended so that groups write their own mystery stories and then compare them.

This unit looks at the roles of teachers and learners in and out of school. The students learn to talk about examinations, different courses, and what they have learnt or would like to learn.

Lesson 1 *Exam time*

Aims: To share experiences about things that can go wrong in examinations, and discuss exam skills and strategies.
To introduce the past continuous tense and contrast it with the past simple.

Language focus

Past continuous and past simple
I **was** just **starting** work on the Saturday morning when the phone **rang**.
When I **started** the exam, all the numbers **were going** round and round.

Skills focus

- **Reading:** instructions for an examination
- **Listening:** for main idea and detail

Vocabulary focus

- Examination rubrics: *read through, fill in, circle, write, name, check, answer*
- Verbs relating to examinations: *revise for, plan, study, have, take, pass, fail, mark*
- Nouns relating to examinations: *exam, test, paper, page, question, answer, result*
- Noun/verb collocations
  answer a question
  enter for an exam

Review and Warmer

Unit 8 Lesson 3 focused on *going to* for future intentions. This structure could be used to introduce the topic of this lesson. Either elicit some sentences from the students about what they are going to do at the end of the English course (if you plan to have a test or exam) or find out from the students if any of them are going to take an exam in another subject, or a driving test.

1

Tell the students that you are going to give them a quick English test now. Introduce the test in Activity 1 as a 'proper' test. Tell the students to work on their own, in complete silence, and with a time limit of three minutes. In fact the test is a trick – most students will probably try to answer all of the questions before they notice the instruction at the end – but do not give this away too soon!

Answers

See Activity 2, below.

2

The results of the test are simple, if unorthodox. Those students who followed the instructions and answered questions 1–4 only, pass. All students who answered all the questions fail.

3

The purpose of this test is therefore not to test the students' English, but to show them how easy it is to lose marks in a test by not following instructions. See if the students can work this out for themselves.

4

This activity provides examples of good and bad ways of dealing with exams. You may wish to pre-teach some of the vocabulary in this activity, eg *study, revise, plan, turn over, miss out,* although students will have met quite a lot of these words already in classroom instructions and the rubrics of this book.

Answers

Happy faces: *3 5*
Sad faces: *1 2 4 6 7*

5

Here the students listen to four people describing exam experiences and match them to the situations described in the last activity. If necessary, you could help the students by telling them that the stories are all 'sad'.
▭ Play the cassette once. Allow the students time to compare answers and then play it again if necessary.

Answers

2 *Annie's brother: situation 7*
3 *Helen: situation 4*
4 *Mike: situation 2*

6

[cassette] Ask the students to look at the tapescript of Mike's story and fill in as many of the gaps as they can from memory. Then play the cassette again so that they can complete it.

Answers

2	*revise*	3	*pass*	4	*starting*
5	*time*	6	*work*	7	*revise*
8	*worked*	9	*numbers*	10	*failed*

The past continuous could also be presented at this stage. (See Practice page 90 Language Summary 1 and the Teacher's notes for Practice page 90.)

7

You could begin this activity by telling an 'exam story' about yourself, or about someone you know. Circulate as the students tell their stories and help with vocabulary and grammar as necessary.

8

This activity recycles vocabulary from the lesson and could be set as an alternative homework task. The students should complete the word gaps alone or in pairs to find the hidden word in the panel.

Answers

```
QUESTIONS
  ANSWER
    SPEND
    TEST
 MARK
 RESULTS
 CHECK
     TIME
  FAIL
 REVISION
 EXAMINATION
   PASS
```

Homework

Tell the students to write this test on a separate sheet of paper and not to write the answers on the test. It can then be used as a review activity in the next lesson.

Practice *page 90*

Language Summary

Ask the students to look back at Lesson 1 Activity 6 (the story about Mike). Ask what Mike was doing on Saturday when the phone rang. (He was just starting work.) Establish the idea of interrupted activity and ask the students to find another example in the passage. (*I **was just sitting** down to do some work on Sunday morning when the phone **rang**.*) Compare this with the third example of the past continuous, (*When I **started** the exam, all the numbers **were still going** round and round in my head.*) where the use is slightly different. Here the action is not interrupted, but occurs both before and after the time Mike walks into the exam room.

Refer the students to the Language Summary which explains the form and use. Point out to the students that the present continuous nearly always occurs together with the past simple.

1

The first exercise practises these two forms together. As this is quite a difficult exercise you may want to do it orally first.

Answers

2	*was interviewing, arrived*	3	*was finishing, went*
4	*arrived, were just going*	5	*was writing, walked*

2

For this activity the students first have to choose the correct verb for each space and then choose the correct form of the, past simple or past continuous. It is quite a difficult activity and would be best done in class, possibly in pairs or groups. First ask the students to choose the correct verbs, and then decide on the form.

If you think the students are likely to find this too difficult, give them the first letter of the verb (infinitive form) in each space as a clue.

Paragraph 1: *was studying*
Paragraph 2: *arrived, was looking, got, was going, made*
Paragraph 3: *told, turned, was driving, stopped, hit*
Paragraph 4: *hit, was crossing, got, stopped, was walking, asked*

3

This activity practises verb-noun and verb-preposition-noun collocations on the topic of examinations.

Answers

Alternative answers are possible but the following are the most common:

check/fail/pass/revise for/take – **an exam**
fail/check/answer/miss out – **a question**
check/miss out – **an answer**

Lesson 2 *Changing places*

Aim: To introduce the language of obligation. This lesson is based on a newspaper article about an English schoolgirl and her father who change places for a day.

Language focus

1 *Have to* and *had to* for obligation
Victoria **had to** do the housework
Dad **didn't have to** wear a skirt

2 *Make, do* and *have*
I hope we **make** a lot of money.
Mr Evans **did** his homework
It was good to **have** a change

Skills focus

- **Reading:** a newspaper article for specific information
- **Speaking:** roleplaying a conversation
- **Listening:** for detail
- **Writing:** a diary entry

Vocabulary focus

- School: *secondary, classmates, lessons, homework*
- Home: *housework, garden, washing up, dinner*
- Charities: *raise/collect money, sell things*

Review

The homework activity set in Lesson 2 (writing an English test) already included an element of 'changing places' as the *students* were writing the test rather than the teacher. To introduce this lesson you could ask the students to give their test to someone else in the class to do, and then tell the students to take back the tests and mark them. This will probably lead to quite a lot of argument, and you will need to circulate and help where necessary. If you have a large or difficult class you may want to take in the tests yourself first and then check them before doing the activity.

1

Introduce the idea of raising money for charity and discuss ways in which it can be done. If the students are not familiar with sponsorship, explain that this is quite a common way of raising money for charity in England, particularly among schoolchildren. People promise to pay a certain amount of money if something is successfully done. Often this is a sporting event, eg running a marathon or swimming, but sometimes people do more unusual things to get sponsored, as in the case described in the newspaper article here.

2

Ask students to read the article quickly and find out what David Evans did to raise money.

Answer

He changed places with his daughter – he went to school for a day and she stayed at home and did the housework.

3

This activity demands closer reading of the article to identify key information. When checking the answers, you should also check that the students have *understood* the information, as they will need this for the roleplay activity.

Answers

1 *Paragraph 1 (Stansted Secondary School)*
2 *Paragraph 4 ('It's very different now, but ten times better.')*
3 *Paragraph 5 (She wears trousers.)*
4 *Paragraph 4 (He's 44.)*
5 *Paragraph 1 (Because one of their classmates changed places with her father.)*
6 *Paragraph 2 (To raise money for charity.)*

4

 This listening gives further input for the roleplay. The students could first predict in pairs what good and bad points they expect Victoria and Mr Evans to mention, and then listen to see how far their predictions were correct.

Answers

	good things	bad things
Victoria's day	seeing dad go off to school	got boring missed her friends
Mr Evans' day	students were nice to him history lesson	going into classroom at first

5

As in previous roleplays, the students can use the information from the lesson but can also add ideas of their own. However, they will need time to prepare. Let student As and student Bs work together first to get ideas together. Help and give ideas and language support as necessary.
Student As (Mr Evans) should think about the different subjects they did on their day at Victoria's school and things that happened during the day.
Student Bs (Victoria) should prepare a list of questions, eg:
Where did you sit?
What was the first lesson?
Was the lesson easy?
What was the next lesson?
Did you like the teachers?

6

If time is short, this could be done for homework.

Answers

2 *at home*
3 *the housework*
4 *in the garden*
5 *the dinner*
6 *washing up*
7 *his homework*
8 *the paper*
9 *a lot of money*

Homework

Students use the diary entry in Activity 6 as a model. Help them with ideas for someone to write about, if necessary.

Practice *page 91*

Language Summary 1

Ask students to look back at Victoria's diary entry in Lesson 2 Activity 6 and to tell you one thing that Victoria **had to** do (*make the dinner*) and one thing she **didn't have to** do (*the washing up*). Check that they understand that in the first example it was necessary for her to make the dinner, and in the second example it wasn't necessary for her to do the washing up.
Elicit the present form (**have to**) and explain that this is often used to talk about rules and regulations.
It is probably best *not* to go into the difference between **must** **have to** at this stage – learners will be readily understood whichever expression they use.

1

This activity recycles the language of examination rubrics from the last lesson.

Answers

2 *have to*
3 *have to*
4 *don't have to*
5 *have to*
6 *don't have to*
7 *have to*
8 *don't have to*

2

This activity contrasts the past and present uses of *have to* by comparing the school lives of Victoria now and her father over thirty years ago.

Answers

1 *Mr Evans didn't have to study a modern language.*
2 *Victoria has to study a modern language.*
3 *Mr Evans had to study Latin.*
4 *Victoria doesn't have to study Latin.*
5 *Mr Evans had to do sport.*
6 *Victoria has to do sport.*
7 *Mr Evans didn't have to go to school on Saturdays.*
8 *Victoria doesn't have to go to school on Saturdays.*
9 *Mr Evans didn't have to learn about computers.*
10 *Victoria has to learn about computers.*

Students could also write sentences about what they *had/didn't have to* do at school (if they have left school) or what they *have to/don't have to* do at school now.

3

Give the students one example of a compound noun – *homework* – and ask if they can remember any others from the lesson, eg *classmates, housework*. Point out that the stress always falls on the first syllable.

Answers

2 *classmate*   3 *classwork*
4 *flatmate*   5 *girlfriend*
6 *homework*   7 *housework*
8 *schoolboy*   9 *schoolfriend*
10 *schoolgirl*   11 *schoolwork*

4

This activity once again stresses the importance of learning words in combinations rather than in isolation. You could introduce it by asking the students to look back again at Victoria's diary and underline each example of *make/do/have* (including past forms), together with the following nouns. The collocations of *make/do/have* are unlikely to be the same in the students' own language and so these expressions have to be learned as 'chunks' of language.
Before the students do Exercise 4, point out that some of the nouns in the box can be used with more than one verb (but there is a difference in meaning).

Answers

make – *a friend, money*
do – *homework, the housework, the shopping, sport*
have – *an exam, a friend, homework, money, a party, a problem*

Check that the students understand the difference between *to make a friend/money* (referring to the beginning of the situation) and *to have a friend/money* (an ongoing state).

Lesson 3 *Something new*

Aims: To look at some of the skills people may learn when they have left school.

Language focus

-ing form or infinitive
I can already **ski**.
I'd like **to learn** to fly a plane.
I'm not interested **in learning** the guitar.

Skills focus

- **Listening:** for the main idea
- **Writing: a** formal letters
- **Reading:** advertisements for courses

Vocabulary focus

- Skills: *use a computer/video camera, drive a car, play the guitar, fly a plane, hang-glide, ski, swim*
- Learning: *learn, teach, instructor, technical side, professional, books, course, class, beginners, qualification, practical, confidence*
- Word formation (nouns and verbs)
  teaching/teacher/to teach
- Formal letters: *Dear Sir/Madam, further information, Yours faithfully*

Review

Before taking the diaries from Lesson 2 in to correct, ask students to talk to their partner for one minute about the content of their diary entry. They should do this from memory and not read the diary aloud. Circulate and monitor.

Warmer

Remind the students of the title of the unit (*Learning for life*) and ask them to tell you all the words they know to do with education and learning. (See the Vocabulary focus for the last two lessons.)

1

Ask the students to look at the list of skills and decide how many of these they can do already and which they would like to learn. Use the pictures to help with vocabulary. Give them the chance to add other skills to the list if they want to. Then tell them to discuss their choices with a partner, using the language in the speech bubbles.

2

 In this part of the cassette three people talk about skills they learnt out of school. Play the cassette and ask students to guess what each person learnt from what they say. All three of them learnt something from the list in Activity 1, not the photographs, so ask the students to focus on the activities in the list. Then, ask students to listen again to find out *why* each person learnt the new skill.

Answers

	Rachel	Sheree	Bruce
What did he/ she learn?	*to ski*	*to use a computer*	*to fly a plane*
Why?	*all her friends could do it*	*important qualification for her job*	*no reason*

3

First, students try to remember who made the statements listed. At the same time, they could deduce vocabulary items from the context or discuss them with their classmates and the teacher.
 Then play the cassette for them to check their answers.

Answers

2 *Sheree*   3 *Rachel*   4 *Bruce*   5 *Sheree*   6 *Bruce*

4

Before starting Activity 4, elicit a list of other skills that people learn on evening or weekend courses, eg painting, cookery. Then ask students to look through the advertisements and underline the different courses mentioned. This is not an intensive reading activity but provides input for the writing activity that follows.

Answers

The courses advertised are:

1 *making home videos*
2 *traditional English cookery*
3 *Latin-American dancing*
4 *driving lessons*

5

This gives the students a model for a simple formal letter, asking for information about courses. You may want to point out the typical layout of this type of letter and the beginnings and endings used when the name is not known.

Before students begin, ask them to find the advertisement for the courses at Hinxton Community College and to tell you the address of the college. Then tell them to continue filling in the gaps in the letter.

Answers

2 *Please*   3 *send*   4 *about*
5 *course*   6 *cookery*   7 *Yours*

Homework

Make sure that students use the model in Activity 5 and lay their letter out correctly.

Practice *page 92*

Language Summary

Refer students back to the three examples in Lesson 3 Activity 1. Point out that when verbs are followed by another verb, the second verb can have one of three different forms: **infinitive without** *to*, **infinitive with** *to* and **-ing form**. Write the three patterns in three columns on the board and ask the students to add other verbs to the columns.

Followed by infinitive without *to*	Followed by infinitive with *to*	Followed by *-ing* form
can	would like	enjoy
should	hope	finish
might	want	to be keen on
could	learn	go (+ sport verb)
will		

1

Exercise 1 recycles the content of Lesson 3 and focuses on the verb forms.

Answers

1 *do, falling, to be*   2 *to use, type, do*   3 *flying, learning, to have*

2

This exercise recycles the vocabulary from Lesson 3 and is a written consolidation of Activity 1.

3

Ask students what the difference is between the words *teach* and *teacher*. Ask students if they can think of any other examples of related verbs and nouns. Then establish the difference between nouns referring to people and other nouns. Exercise 3 explores this with some examples from the lesson.

Answers

Noun	Noun (person)	Verb
teaching	*teacher*	teach
profession	*professional*	–
instruction	instructor	instruct
beginning	*beginner*	*begin*
introduction	–	*introduce*
information	–	inform
advertisement	–	advertise

4

Exercise 4 develops proof-reading skills so that students can check their own work for spelling and grammar mistakes.

Answers

Grammar mistakes: could you *send* me; I'm interested *in going*
Spelling mistakes: *Please, information, holidays, interested, January*

The theme of this unit is celebrations, either for special occasions, such as birthdays and weddings, or for the end of something, such as a course. This develops in the third lesson into the idea of a celebration for the end of the century.

Lesson 1 *What a lovely present!*

Aims: To teach the common functional expressions used for special occasions and the language for thanking people, both spoken and written.

Language focus

1 Expressions for special occasions:
   Happy birthday!
   Congratulations!

2 Relative clauses with *who*
   Which card would you send to Helen, **who** is 21 years old today?

Skills focus

- **Listening:** to short dialogues for specific information and for the language used to say thank you
- **Writing:** a letter of thanks

Vocabulary focus

- Typical presents: *pot plant, photograph album, cake, compact disc, belt, toy animal*
- Adjectives to describe presents: *lovely, sweet, beautiful, great, delicious*
- Special occasions: *birthday, wedding, anniversary*

Review

Ask the students to get into groups according to the course they wrote about in the letter for homework. Ask them to compare their letters while you circulate to monitor and correct.

Warmer

You could ask students to make a line around your classroom in the order of their birthdays – starting with January and ending with December. Then elicit what happens on your birthday: *Do you receive presents? How do you celebrate? Which birthdays are the most important?*

1

Ask students to look at the five cards in Activity 1 and match them to the people. Encourage them to use the pictures to help them to deduce the vocabulary.

Answers

1 *Helen: the card in front on the left.*
2 *Paul: the 'get well soon' card.*
3 *Mike and Emma: 'on your wedding day'.*
4 *Bruce and Jan: the card in the middle in the front.*
5 *John and Marjorie: 'your golden anniversary'.*

In Britain, different wedding anniversaries are associated with different symbols, often precious stones or metals. 'Silver' is 25 years, 'gold' is 50, and 'diamond' is 60. You could find out if your students have similar traditions.

2

Ask the students on which of these occasions you might give a present. Elicit some typical presents. Then ask students to look at the two lists of words and match them to form compound nouns or adjective-noun combinations.

Answers

*pot plant   compact disc   bedside lamp   leather belt
wine glasses   toy animal   photograph album*

3

Ask students to work in pairs and decide which of the presents from Activity 2 they would choose for the people in Activity 1. Make sure that they only complete column 1 at this stage.
⏹ Next, play the cassette and tell them to note down which presents the people actually received. Play the cassette again if necessary.

Answers

Helen:	leather belt
Paul:	chocolate cake
Mike and Emma:	bedside lamp
Bruce and Jan:	toy animal
John and Marjorie:	wine glasses

4

⏹ Students now listen to the same part of the cassette and focus on the language items. Ask them to tick the expressions they hear on the cassette.
After playing the cassette once, ask them to compare their answers in pairs, then play the cassette again if necessary. Point out that British people tend to use two sentences when they are thanking someone, one to say thank you directly and one to add something about the present.

Answers

- ✓ Happy birthday!
- ✓ Thank you.
- ☐ I like it.
- ✓ It's lovely.
- ✓ How are you feeling?
- ✓ That's great.
- ✓ Thanks a lot.
- ✓ Congratulations!
- ☐ Thanks.
- ✓ Thank you very much.
- ☐ That's really kind of you
- ✓ It's just what we wanted.
- ✓ Isn't that sweet!
- ☐ Aren't they beautiful!
- ☐ You're very kind.

5

Students work in pairs in this activity, but they think of a present individually first. They then give the 'present' to their partner. Their partner should thank them, using two or three expressions from Activity 4.

6

Students are now introduced to more lengthy thank you letters. Ask students to decide which sentences belong to which letter, and then tell them to decide on the order of the sentences.

Answers

Dear Sarah
7 *Thank you very much for coming to see me and for bringing me that delicious chocolate cake.*
6 *I really enjoyed it – the food here is horrible!*
2 *It was good to see you and to hear how people at work are getting on without me.*
8 *I hope I'll be home again soon.*
9 *Thanks very much again.*

Dear Alison
1 *Sorry you couldn't come to the party but thank you very much for the belt.*
4 *It looks great with my black jeans.*
3 *Come and see me again soon – I've got lots of news and some new things to show you.*
5 *Many thanks again for the belt.*

After checking, look briefly at the model format for a letter of thanks: opening, thanks for the present, a sentence about the present, a more general sentence, repeated thanks, ending. Finally ask students to identify which person from Activity 1 wrote each letter and to write in the names at the ends of the letters.

Answers

Letter A is from Paul. *Letter B is from Helen.*

Homework

Make sure that students follow the **model given** and discussed in Activity 6.

Practice *page 93*

1

Refer students back to Lesson 1 Activity 1.
Revise the expressions used for the occasions shown on the cards. In Exercise 1 students will meet this functional language together with a few more expressions and more situations. They could do this exercise in pairs.

Answers

| 2 *a* | 3 *a* | 4 *b* | 5 *c* | 6 *c* |

2

This exercise recycles the same language but this time the students match the two parts of a dialogue. In each dialogue, the occasion being talked about is clear.

Answers

| 2 *b* | 3 *g* | 4 *h* | 5 *a* | 6 *f* | 7 *c* | 8 *e* |

Students could use these dialogues for oral practice. Circulate while they work in pairs, encouraging them to use suitable expressions and intonation as they read out the dialogues.

Language Summary 2

You could remind students about relative clauses with **where**, which they looked at in Unit 8 Lesson 2; '*See the world*' and then compare those examples with the examples of relative clauses with **who** in Language Summary 2.
Explain that the difference is that **where** refers to places and **who** refers to people. Otherwise, they follow the same pattern and perform the same function. Do not go into the terminology of non-defining relative clauses at this stage.

3

Ask students to do Exercise 3. You may prefer to do it orally, or to let the students work in pairs.

Answers

2 The chocolate cake was for Paul, *who was in hospital.*
3 The bedside lamp was for Mike and Emma, *who were getting married.*
4 The toy animal was for Jan and Bruce, *who had a new baby.*
5 The wine glasses were for John and Marjorie, *who got married exactly 50 years ago.*
6 The compact disc was for Antonio, *who had a new CD player.*
7 The photograph album was for Rafael, *who had a new camera.*

Lesson 2 *Party time*

Aim: To explore the theme of parties and their different aspects – food and drink, invitations, arrangements, guests

Language focus

1 Ways of describing people
  The girl **who lives next door** works in a dress shop.
  The man **in the striped sweater** is called Steve.
  The girl **with short fair hair** is 21 today.

2 Invitations
  Would you like to come?
  Can you come at about eight?

Skills focus

- **Listening:** to a phone conversation for specific information, and listening to a talk for detail
- **Speaking:** roleplaying a phone conversation
- **Reading:** information about people in order to identify them

Vocabulary focus

- Parties: *invitation, food, drink, music, dancing, juke box*
- Food and drink: *bread, cheese, salad, apples, birthday cake, beer, wine, soft drinks*
- Physical description: *glasses, moustache, short hair, fair hair*
- Clothes and accessories: *black jeans, T-shirt, striped sweater, ear-ring, white shirt*

Review

Tell the students to deliver the letter they wrote for homework (Unit 10 Lesson 1) to the person who gave them the present. Encourage the students to read and check the letters they receive. Circulate and answer questions as necessary.

Warmer

Remind the students of Helen, who featured in Unit 10 Lesson 1. Elicit the occasion she was celebrating (21st birthday – this is an important birthday in Britain) and discuss ways of celebrating an important birthday, and the types of arrangements you need to make for a big party, eg music, invitations, etc.
If possible, bring in, or ask students to bring in, pictures of party food and drinks, eg crisps, olives, cakes, champagne.

1

Ask students to work in pairs or groups and make a list of party food and drink. Circulate and help the groups with vocabulary and spelling. You may find pictures useful and could also encourage the students to use dictionaries.

2

This is a typical format for a party invitation. You may want to point out the layout and organization of both the invitation and the envelope to students if written conventions are different in their countries. Elicit from the students the type of information they are listening for (date, time, names and addresses) and then play the cassette, twice if necessary.

Answers

On *(Saturday) 6th April*
At *8.00*
Address *119 Hanger Lane, Leeds*
From *Helen*

Baz Wilson
117 College Road
Leeds
LS17 2HN

3

Students now hear Helen talking about the arrangements for her 21st birthday party and make notes about the topics listed. You could begin by discussing what they expect to hear for each topic. As there are quite a lot of details to catch, students will need to compare ideas and listen at least twice.

Answers

2 food: *cheese, (French) bread, crisps, pizza, salad*
3 drink: *beer, wine, soft drinks, orange juice*
4 music: *a juke box with 60s and 70s music, disco, rock 'n' roll, salsa, pop, (a bit of everything)*
5 activities: *dancing*

4

This is a puzzle in which students have to read and record the information in order to match the names with details of physical appearance, occupations and relationships. It is probably best done individually and then checked in pairs or groups.

Answers

Name	Description	Occupation	Who they are
Helen	long fair hair		
Kathryn	black jeans and T-shirt	post-graduate student	Helen's sister
Phil	dark hair	German student	old friend of Helen's
Baz	short hair, ear-ring	makes videos	Kathryn's ex-boyfriend
Janet	white shirt	works in a dress shop	lives next door
Steve	striped sweater	sells cars	married to Janet

5

The students now roleplay a phone conversation which takes place between Helen and Phil after the party. Allocate roles to the students and give them time to prepare their roles. Circulate and help as necessary.
Then ask students to do the roleplay. Circulate and then choose one or two pairs to perform the roleplay to the class.

Homework

When setting the homework, elicit the types of things you might record in a diary: *the reason for the party, the atmosphere at the party, anyone you particularly liked, what you talked to him/her about,* etc.

Practice *page 94*

Language Summary 1

Refer the students back to Lesson 2 Activity 4. Ask them to underline any phrases they can find beginning with *who*, *with* or *in*. Elicit the function of these phrases (to describe people). Then look at Language Summary 1 for more detail of how these phrases are used.

1

Ask students to do Exercise 1, which practises the receptive use of these structures.

Answers

a Manuel	*b Yuko*	*c Gabriel*
d Margarita	*e Carlos*	*f Aki*

2

Before the students do Exercise 2, you could ask them to decide in pairs how to use the phrases in the box, ie with *who*, *with* or *in*. They then write complete sentences as in the example.

Answers

2 *The student who is sitting down is called* Marco.
3 *The student with a scarf is called* Helga.
4 *The student with fair hair is called* Christina.
5 *The student in the striped shirt is called* Hassan.
6 *The student with a moustache is called* Mehmet.

Language Summary 2

Refer the students back to Lesson 2 Activity 2, where Helen phoned Phil to invite him to her party. You could play the cassette again and ask the students to listen and note down the language Helen uses to invite him to the party. Then tell them to compare what they have written with the examples given in Language Summary 2, before doing Exercise 3.

3

Answers

2 *Would you like to come to my graduation?*
3 *Would you like to come to our wedding?*

This exercise could be extended to an oral activity in which students invite each other to different events. For this, it would also be useful to teach ways of accepting invitations, eg *I'd love to, That'd be great,* and of refusing them, eg *I'm really sorry, I'm already busy, I'm afraid I can't, I'm doing something else.*

Lesson 3 *It's the end*

Aims: To talk about celebrations marking the end of events/life stages and relate these to the Millennium – the end of the century.

Language focus

1 Review of verb forms
  Another society **has** a different project.
  As long ago as 1974 a British company **booked** the Albert Hall in London.
  They **will** spend New Year's Eve at the Pyramids.

2 Talking about dates and times – more prepositions
  On 6th April.
  At twelve o'clock.
  In the year 2000.

Skills focus

- **Reading:** for the main idea and detail
- **Speaking:** planning a celebration

Vocabulary focus

- Places/events: *picnic, club, theatre, restaurant, dance*
- Planning celebrations: *food, drink, music*
- Planning: *plan, to book, project, event*

Review

Ask a few students to read their diary entries from lesson 2 to the class. Then take them in to correct.
You could extend the activity by grouping together those students who chose the same person to write about, and letting them compare ideas to see if they wrote about the same things.

1

Ask students to work in groups and talk about a celebration they had, eg the reason for the celebration, what they did, etc. They report back orally.

2

Ask students to do Activity 2 in pairs.

Answers

> *go out for a drink, a meal*
> *go to a club, the theatre, a restaurant, the cinema, a disco, a dance*

3

 Play the cassette and ask students to identify the reasons for celebrations. Then play the cassette again so that they can complete the second column.

Answers

1	*end of school*	*all went to a club together*
2	*end of German course*	*had a party at the teacher's house*
3	*end of university*	*had a formal dance*
4	*new job*	*went out for a drink with friends and flatmates*
5	*last day at work*	*went to a restaurant with friends, then went to a disco*

4

Ask students to read the text through quickly to identify the reason for the celebration. (December 31st 1999.) Discuss the different ways this is referred to: *New Year's Eve 1999, The Millennium, the Year 2000.*

5

Students match the main topics of the article to the paragraphs.

Answers

2 *paragraph 4*
3 *paragraph 2*
4 *paragraph 3*
5 *paragraph 1*

6

To prepare for this activity, teach the vocabulary connected with planning from the reading passage: *to plan, to book, to talk about doing something, a project*. Also check that students understand the vocabulary in the table.

Answers

Event	Definite?	Not definite?
2 Tree planting	✓	
3 World TV linkup		✓
4 Buying the first TV advert of 2000		✓
5 Royal Albert Hall Party	✓	

Check that the students have understood the language in the passage. 2 is definite because it is already planned: *They plan to plant trees*. 3 is not definite: *Some people think we may see ...* .4 *Businesses are talking about buying ...* 5 *a British company booked*.

7

Ask students to work in groups and do whichever activity they prefer. Ask each group to prepare a poster with the details of their celebration on it.

Practice *page 95*

1

As this is a revision activity, you could ask students to do Exercise 1 before looking at the Language Summary. Then refer back to earlier lessons and language summaries for remedial work as necessary.

Answers

2 *invited*
3 *came*
4 *was*
5 *was just starting*
6 *had*
7 *are meeting*
8 *know*
9 *will be*
10 *is*
11 *will be*

Language Summary

You could write the prepositions *at*, *in* and *on* on the board and then see if students can remember which one you use with dates (such as ***December 31st 1999***), which one with days of the week (eg ***Monday***) and which one with times (eg ***midnight/12.00***).
Then introduce the use of *at* with holidays, eg *at Christmas*, and the use of *in* with years, eg *in 1996, in the year 2000*.

2

Students can then do Exercise 2, which is very controlled.

Answers

at	in	on
11.00	*the year 2000*	*December 31st 1999*
5.30	*2001*	*New Year's Eve*
Christmas	*2010*	*Tuesday afternoons*

3

This is a more personalized activity practising the same language. Students can compare answers in pairs or groups, or present them as a survey.

4

This is a final vocabulary review activity and can be done in groups. Students could go on to produce more extended vocabulary networks if they wanted to. See the vocabulary network in Unit 1 Lesson 2 Practice page 67 as an example.

Section 1: Comprehension
[20 marks]

1 a Read the passage. What is special about Tracy Hinton? Tick (✓) the best answer. [2 marks]

1 She takes part in competitions with a partner. ☐
2 She took part in the European championships. ☐
3 She's a very good runner who can't see. ☐

BLINDING SUCCESS!

Tracy Hinton is a European champion – with gold medals in the 100, 200 and 400 metres. But many people don't know of her. And this is because she is blind. We interviewed Tracy about her amazing story.

When did you start running?
I started running at school when I was eleven. I could see until I was four. Then I went blind and I started going to a school for the blind. At first running was quite frightening. But our teachers were very good and they helped me.

How do blind people run in races?
We have a 'seeing partner', someone who runs next to us. This person must be a good runner too! To keep together, we hold a piece of leather in our hands. You form a close relationship with your partner – this person is your eyes.

What other sports can blind people do?
There are lots. Swimming is good because it's something you can do all by yourself. There are all sorts of games that blind people can play – even golf and archery. There's also goalball, which is a sport just for people who can't see. It's only fast games like tennis which we can't take part in.

Why don't people know about blind athletes?
Because we are not on TV or in the newspapers very much. As a result, we don't get any money from sponsors. We have to pay most of the costs ourselves. I want to take part in this year's World Championships, for example, but it's going to cost me £400.

Do you ever run against people who can see?
Oh, yes. I couldn't run against some of our best men runners – their times will always be better than mine. But in local competitions I run against people who can see. At first they were very surprised when they saw me at the start. But now they're getting used to the idea.

What sporting advice can you give to young blind people?
Have a go! Taking part in competitions is hard and often the help you need isn't there. But don't be put off – you just have to keep going.

b Are these sentences true or false? Write T or F in the box. [10 marks]

Example: Tracy is very famous. ☐F☐
1 Tracy won three gold medals. ☐
2 Tracy started running before she went blind. ☐
3 Her running partner is blind too. ☐
4 Tracy is faster than all the best men runners in Britain. ☐
5 She never runs against people who can see. ☐

c Write answers to these questions about the passage. You do not need to write complete sentences. [8 marks]

1 Who helped Tracy become interested in running?
_____

2 Why is swimming good for blind people?
_____

3 Why can't blind people play tennis?
_____

4 Who will pay if Tracy takes part in the World Championships?
_____

Section 2: Communication
[20 marks]

2 Write questions for these answers.

Example: *What do you do?* _____
I'm a student. I'm studying music.
1 _____
I'm 23. It was my birthday last week.
2 _____
No, I haven't. But I've got a motorbike.
3 _____
I like casual clothes – jeans and T-shirts.
4 _____
No, there isn't. But you can buy food in the shop.
5 _____
I don't like it. I prefer classical music.
6 _____
I'm sorry, I can't. I haven't got a watch.
7 _____
For my last holiday? I went skiing in France.
8 _____
Yes, of course. It's 51321. That's the fax number too.
9 _____
My sister? She's tall and slim and she's got red hair.
10 _____
I'm going shopping on Saturday and on Sunday I think I'll stay at home.

Section 3: Language [20 marks]

3 a **Choose ten of these words to complete the first ten spaces in the conversation. Underline each word you choose. [10 marks]**

Example: A be B <u>do</u> C work
1 A a B an C the
2 A at B in C on
3 A work B working C works
4 A very B more C most
5 A hours B time C times
6 A can B have C must
7 A after B during C until
8 A many B much C well
9 A How B What C Which
10 A last B next C this

b **Complete the last ten spaces with your own words. Write one word in each space. [10 marks]**

RICHARD: What do you _____*do*_____ , Valerie?

VALERIE: I'm (1)_____ receptionist. I work in a hotel (2)_____ the centre of London.

RICHARD: Do you like (3)_____ in a hotel?

VALERIE: It's (4)_____ interesting than my last job – I worked in a shop. But I work longer (5)_____ now. And I often (6)_____ to work in the evenings. Sometimes I don't finish (7)_____ midnight. I don't like that very (8)_____ .

RICHARD: I'm not surprised. (9) _____ do you spend your free time?

VALERIE: I'm doing a language course (10)_____ month and I'm enjoying that. I'm learning a little Italian so that I (11)_____ understand our Italian guests.

RICHARD: What about the (12)_____ you work with? Are they nice?

VALERIE: They're all very friendly. I (13)_____ go out with Jane when we're both free. We go to a sports centre, (14)_____ we play squash.

RICHARD: Who's Jane?

VALERIE: She's a new girl (15)_____ works in the kitchen. She's from Wellington. She came to Britain about three months (16)_____ .

RICHARD: Wellington's in New Zealand, (17)_____ it?

VALERIE: Yes, that's right. I'd like (18)_____ go there. I (19)_____ go with Jane next summer. We're already beginning to (20)_____ plans.

Section 4: Writing [20 marks]

4 **You recently stayed with a friend for a few days. Write and thank your friend after your visit.**

Dear _____

_____

_____

_____

_____

_____

_____

_____

_____

_____

_____

_____

_____

_____

_____

PHOTOCOPIABLE

To the Teacher

Each of the four levels of *Accelerate* is accompanied by a test, which consists of:

- a *To the teacher* section
- photocopiable worksheets for students
- an answer key

The tests can serve two purposes.

1 Diagnostic. The tests can be used to enable the teacher to assess the level of a class as a whole and to identify general areas of weakness before students begin the course.

2 Achievement. The tests can be used to allow both students and teacher to identify progress made during the course. Students can repeat the test upon completion of their course even if they have already taken the same test at the beginnning; in this way they can assess their improvement.

Each test is divided into six parts. These are:

1 Comprehension
2 Communicaton
3 Language
4 Writing
5 Dictation (optional)
6 Oral task (optional)

Each section of the test carries 20 marks. The marks can be adjusted by the teacher, with greater or less emphasis given to particular sections.

Optional Section 5: Dictation
[20 marks]

Tell students that you are going to dictate five sentences. Explain that you will read each sentence three times. First, read each sentence at normal speed. Then read the sentences slowly, breaking them up into phrases. Finally, read the sentences once more at normal speed.

4 marks for each sentence. Deduct one mark for each mistake.

1 I never go to discos on my own.
2 He left school when he was fifteen.
3 A friend is someone who shares your problems.
4 She couldn't speak English before she came here.
5 He was doing his homework when the phone began to ring.

Optional Section 6: Speaking Task [20 marks]

Students work in pairs. Give each student a copy of the task. If you wish, you could try to record each conversation so that you can assess students' work at a later point in time.

Tell students what you will take into consideration when assessing their oral work. Criteria should include:

- fluency: speaking without too much hesitation [4 marks]
- grammatical accuracy: speaking without too many mis takes [4 marks]
- pronunciation: making individual sounds correctly, using stress, rhythm and intonation appropriately [4 marks]
- vocabulary: using a wide range of appropriate vocabulary [4 marks]
- communication: being able to ask questions, give opinions/advice etc [4 marks]

Speaking Task

What do you do in your free time? Choose three of your hobbies and be prepared to tell your partner about your interest in these things.

Work with your partner. Find out how your partner spends his or her free time. Give your own opinion of your partner's hobbies. Find out if you have anything in common.

Section 1: Comprehension
[20 marks]

1 a 2 marks for the correct answer.

    3

  b 10 marks: 2 marks for each correct answer.

    1 T   2 F   3 F   4 F   5 F

  c 8 marks: 2 marks for each correct answer. Do not deduct marks for notes rather than complete sentences. Suggestions include:

    1 her teachers
    2 They can do it by themselves./You can do it by yourself.
    3 Too fast
    4 Tracy/She will

Section 2: Communication
[20 marks]

2   2 marks for each question. Deduct one mark for each major mistake. For instance, ignore small spelling mistakes, unless the word is incomprehensible. Any correct question is acceptable. Suggestions include:

    1 How old are you?
    2 Have you got a car?
    3 What clothes do you like (wearing)?
    4 Is there a restaurant (near here)?
    5 Do you like reggae/rock music etc?/How do you feel about reggae etc?
    6 Can you tell me the time?
    7 What did you do for your last holiday?/Where did you go for your last holiday?
    8 Can/May I have your phone number?/Can you give me your phone number?
    9 What does your sister look like?
  10 What are you doing at the weekend?/What are you going to do at the weekend?/What are your plans for the weekend?

Section 3: Language [20 marks]

3 a 10 marks: 1 mark for each correct answer.

    1 a   2 in   3 working
    4 more   5 hours   6 have
    7 until   8 much   9 How
  10 this

  b 10 marks: 1 mark for each appropriate answer. Suggestions include:

  11 can/will
  12 people/receptionists/staff
  13 always/frequently/occasionally/often/sometimes/usually
  14 and/where
  15 who
  16 ago
  17 isn't
  18 to
  19 could/may/might
  20 make

Section 4: Writing [20 marks]

You might like to tell students what you will take into consideration when marking their written work. Criteria should include:

- efficient communication of meaning [7 marks]
- grammatical accuracy [7 marks]
- coherence in the ordering or the information or ideas [3 marks]
- capitalisation and punctuation [3 marks]

It is probably better not to use a rigid marking system with the written part of the test. If, for example, you always deduct a mark for a grammatical mistake, you may find that are over-penalising students who write a lot or who take risks. Deduct marks if students haven't written the minimum number of sentences stated in the test.

Unit 1, Lesson 1, Activity 2

Pete: Well, I've got a motorbike, but I haven't got a car. At home I've got a guitar, and a computer, but I haven't got a television. I've got a cat. He's called Sasha, and a dog called Otto.

Unit 1, Lesson 1, Activity 4

Interviewer: Excuse me, could I ask you a few questions, please?
Pete: Er … OK.
Interviewer: First of all, what's your name, please?
Pete: Pete Ford.
Interviewer: And … how old are you?
Pete: I'm 22.
Interviewer: Where do you live?
Pete: I live in London.
Interviewer: And what do you do?
Pete: I'm a student.
Interviewer: Do you like sport?
Pete: Yes, especially football.
Interviewer: And have you got a car?
Pete: No, I haven't, but I've got a motorbike.
Interviewer: That's all. Thank you very much.
Pete: That's OK.

Unit 1, Lesson 2, Activity 3

Emma: Well, Mike's got short, fair hair and glasses. He's quite tall, and he's got blue eyes, really nice eyes. And his clothes, well, he wears quite a lot of blue, and usually jeans, and he likes sport a lot. He does a lot of sport.

Unit 1, Lesson 2, Activity 4

Mike: What have Emma and I got in common? Well, quite a lot really I suppose. Well, we've both got glasses for a start and we're both quite tall. I'm 24 and she's 22, so we're different ages, and we live in different places. She lives in Oxford and I live in London. We're both students, but she's studying art and I'm studying business. What else? Well she's got dark eyes but my eyes aren't dark, they're blue, and she likes wearing black, lots of her clothes are black, while I wear blue mostly, but we both like wearing jeans. I like sport but Emma doesn't, but we both quite like watching television sometimes. And reading, we both like reading magazines like 'Profile'.

Unit 1, Lesson 3, Activity 3

Well, I think a good engineer is clever, especially at maths and science, and a practical sort of person, and they've got to be good with numbers of course.
And an art teacher, well an art teacher's got to be artistic, and if they're a teacher they've got to be good with people, but … well, I think an art teacher has to be quite practical as well. What about a doctor? Well, I'd go for clever again, and he or she's working with people all the time so they've got to be good with people, and then I think a good doctor is kind as well.
Well a bank manager's obviously good with numbers, and they need to be good with people too, and the third thing for a bank manager, or for any manager, is, I think, they have to be independent, because they're the manager, they're in charge.

Unit 2, Lesson 2, Activity 3

Jacky: My dream car … I'd have something really fast, and very expensive, definitely a GOOD car – yes, my dream car would be a Testarossa
Dominic: Well I haven't got a car, but my dream would be to have a jeep because they're really practical, and they're strong, and so they're safe as well.

Unit 2, Lesson 3, Activities 2 and 3

1 – Annie
I want to fly to Florida on Concorde and go to Disneyworld.

2 – Rachel
I want to drive around in a Porsche and buy lots of expensive clothes.

3 – Ben
I want to go back in time millions of years and see the dinosaurs.

4 – Mike
I want to take part in the Olympic games and win a medal.

5 – Jacky
I want to go to bed with a good book and a box of chocolates, and sleep for hours.

Unit 3, Lesson 1, Activity 1

1–5 What do you call this sort of music?

Unit 3, Lesson 1, Activities 2 and 3

Interviewer: How do you feel about disco music? Do you like it?
Helen: Yes, I think it's great.
Phil: Disco? Oh, no. I don't like it at all.
Interviewer: And how about classical music?
Helen: Oh, yes, I like it a lot
Interviewer: How about you, Phil?
Phil: No, I don't like it.
Interviewer: And how do you feel about reggae?
Helen: Um … It's OK. I don't mind it.
Phil: It's alright.
Interviewer: How about jazz?
Helen: I'm not very keen on it.
Phil: Yeah, it … it's alright. It's OK I suppose.
Interviewer: And how do you feel about heavy metal?
Helen: Oh, I love it!
Phil: Yes, it's great!

Unit 3, Lesson 2, Activities 1 and 2

1
Man 1: Do you do any sport?
Woman 1: I go jogging in the mornings

2
Man 2: Do you do any sport?
Man 3: I often go swimming at the weekend.

3
Woman 2: Do you do any sport?
Man 4: Well, I play cricket. I'm in the school team.

4
Woman 3: Do you do any sport?
Woman 4: I do gymnastics at school but I'm not very keen on it.

5
Woman 5: Do you do any sport?
Man 5: I play football every weekend.

6
Man 6: Do you do any sport?
Woman 6: I do aerobics on Saturday mornings.

7
Man 7: Do you do any sport?
Man 8: I quite like to play a game of golf or two when I'm on holiday.

8
Woman 7: Do you do any sport?
Woman 8: Well, we go skiing in the winter, usually in Switzerland, or sometimes in … France.

9
Man 9: Do you do any sport?
Woman 9: I play basketball for the team. We're playing in a match on Sunday.

10
Woman 10: Do you do any sport?
Man 10: Sometimes I … I play tennis, but I'm …
I'm not very good.

11
Woman 11: Do you do any sport?
Man 11: Yes, I play volleyball. A lot of people in my country play it.

Unit 3, Lesson 3, Activity 3

Emma: Put the helmet on. What can you see?
Mike: I can see a room.
Emma: What's in front of you?
Mike: Er … a window, with curtains.
Emma: Now turn your head to the left. What can you see there?
Mike: There's a picture on the wall.
Emma: Now turn your head to the right. What's there?
Mike: There's a door.

Unit 3, Lesson 3, Activity 4

Emma: Now look ahead again … look at the window and press the button on your hand set.
Mike: Oh … I'm going towards the window … the curtains are opening. There are some birds in the sky … one bird is coming closer … it's getting bigger … help!
Emma: Press the other button on the handset.
Mike: Oh, um … now I'm going away from the window. Now I'm turning my head to look at the picture on my left. It's a picture of the sea. There's a ship on the sea. It's … it's getting bigger and, now … now I'm on the ship. The sea's going up and down and now … I'm … I'm IN the sea. The, um … the fish are coming up close to look at me. Um … I'm pressing the button again and I'm going up, away from the fish, back onto the ship and then back into the room.
Right behind me there's a door in the wall. The door is closed. I'm turning round to look at the door …

Unit 3, Lesson 3, Activity 5

Now I'm turning my head to look at the picture on my left. It's a picture of the sea. There's a ship on the sea. It's … it's getting bigger and now … now I'm on the ship. The sea's going up and down and now I'm … I'm IN the sea. The, um … the fish are coming up close to look at me. Um … I'm pressing the button again and I'm going up, away from the fish, back onto the ship and then back into the room.
Right behind me there's a door in the wall. The door is closed. I'm turning round to look at the door …

Unit 4, Lesson 1, Activities 3 and 4

Man: Excuse me, is this Peter's class?
Woman: Yes, I think so.
Man: Is this seat free?
Woman: Yes of course. Oh, is that the textbook for this class? Can I have a look?
Man: Sure.
Woman: Mmmm. It's quite difficult, isn't it?
Man: Yes it is, isn't it?

Unit 4, Lesson 2, Activity 3

1
I use it to send letters and pictures to our office in New York.

2
I use it all the time to find and store information and to write letters.

3
I like having it in case I break down when I'm driving at night.

4
When I get home I listen to it to find out if I got any phone calls during the day.

Unit 4, Lesson 2, Activities 5 and 6

Message 1
Scott: Er … hello. I'm phoning about your advertisement. Um … well, you're looking for a group it said and er … well, I might be able to help. The thing is I play in a rock group at the moment. Um … we're looking for a singer who can also play bass guitar. We're based in Manchester … um … well, maybe you could ring me back to talk about the details. I'm on 061-347 7693. Oh … and my name's Scott … Scott Wrigley. Bye.

Message 2
Rachel: I'm ringing to answer your advert. I'm a 24-year-old and I desperately need a holiday. I'm starting a new job in September but I'm free until then. I'd like to join you for a trip … India or Australia preferably! Do you think we'd get on? If so, ring me back. … I'm Rachel and my number's 0799 523659.

Message 3
Jacky: Hello, I'm phoning about your advertisement for an English host family. My husband and I offer a room to students for £65 a week. We usually provide breakfast and an evening meal for that … what else is important … well, we've got three children and … um, we enjoy having students … we treat them as one of the family!

Unit 4, Lesson 3, Activity 1

Mike: Excuse me, Mrs Springer. Could I have a quick word?
Mrs Springer: Yes, certainly. What's the problem?
Mike: Er … well, it's … it's just that I'm a bit worried about the work for Simpsons. Um … it has to be done by Friday or we lose the order.

Unit 4, Lesson 3, Activity 4

Interviewer: Mike, do you talk to people about politics?
Mike: Well not a lot but , er … sometimes … My sister is interested in politics, so I talk to her mostly.
Interviewer: And what about the past? Who do you talk … ?
Mike: <u>My</u> past?
Interviewer: Yes.
Mike: Well no-one really. I don't think about the past much.
Interviewer: And money? Do you talk to other people about money?
Mike: Oh yes, I talk about money to anybody, … everybody.
Interviewer: Oh and relationships? Do you talk about them?
Mike: Yes, to friends … only close friends though.
Interviewer: And is it the same for health or … ?
Mike: Health? Oh, I don't know … I suppose I talk to mum. It depends.

Interviewer: Emma, do you talk about politics much?
Emma: Yes, to my family – we all talk about politics a lot – we don't agree and we argue a lot!
Interviewer: And do you talk much about the past?
Emma: Yes … when I'm with my friends, especially old school friends.
Interviewer: And what about money? Who do you talk to about that?
Emma: Oh, people at college, all the time!
Interviewer: What about relationships? Who do you talk to about relationships?
Emma: Not many people, but sometimes my brother.
Interviewer: And last of all, health. I mean, if you don't feel well or you're worried about a health problem, who do you talk to?
Emma: I suppose I talk to my doctor, yes, my doctor, she's very nice.

Unit 5, Lesson 1, Activity 3

Well in 1986 I left College and I got a job as a TV journalist. Umm, and in 1988, I got engaged, but unfortunately things did not work out very well … so in 1989 I moved to another town and I got a job as a teacher, teaching English. Then, in 1991, I went to England to do a course for a year. After that, I went back to Mozambique and I worked as a teacher and disc jockey, and in 1993 I got married.

Unit 5, Lesson 3, Activities 1 and 2

Ganesh Sittampalam, from Surbiton, South London, yesterday became Britain's youngest first class maths graduate. Ganesh, who was only eleven years old when he started university, went to university one day a week and did ordinary lessons at school with his friends the rest of the time. In his free time, Ganesh watches television and plays football with friends of his own age. He said yesterday, 'I'm happy because I've done it, not because of my age.'

Unit 5, Lesson 3, Activity 3

In Britain the law is that at the age of sixteen you can leave school, and you can get married if you have your parents' permission. You can also ride a moped, and you can buy cigarettes. At seventeen you can ride a motorbike or drive a car. At eighteen you are legally an adult. You can buy alcoholic drinks and get married – without your parents' permission.

Unit 6, Lesson 1, Activity 1

Phil: 'I make new friends quickly' … yes, I think I do. How about you, Helen?
Helen: No, no I don't. It takes me quite a long time usually. How about the next one? 'I tell my close friends everything'.
Phil: No, certainly not.
Helen: Don't you? Not even close friends? I think I tell my closest friends just about everything.
Phil: 'I laugh a lot with my friends'. Yes, that's true for me.
Helen: Yes, me too. How about number four?
Phil: Well, I like my brother a lot but he's not my best friend. No, my best friend's not in my family.
Helen: No, I like my family but my best friend isn't in my family either.
Phil: Number five … 'I sometimes argue with my friends'. No, that's not me. You don't argue either, do you?
Helen: Well, actually I do argue sometimes, yes.
Phil: Oh, really? And writing letters. No, I don't.
Helen: I do.
Phil: How about the last one? What do you think?
Helen: No, I don't really think it's possible. Not just friends.
Phil: What, never? Oh, I do. I definitely think it's possible.

Unit 6, Lesson 2, Activity 5

Take a piece of paper.
First, write the name of a famous woman, then fold the paper over and pass it to the person on your left.
On the paper you receive, write 'met' and the name of a famous man. Then fold the paper over and pass it to the person on your left.
On the next paper you receive, write 'in' 'at' or 'on' and the name of a place. Fold the paper over again and pass it to your left.
On the paper you receive, write 'She said …' and then write something the woman says. Pass the paper on.
Repeat the last step, but this time write 'He said …' and the man's reply. Pass the paper on.
Finally, write 'The result was …' and write what happened to the two people.

Unit 6, Lesson 3, Activity 2

Well, I've got two children at university now but they used to live with us and we got on very well except for one or two problems. One, their bedrooms were so untidy all the time, I … I could never get them to tidy their bedrooms and the other thing is – they're both vegetarian. That didn't cause much of a problem with us because we don't eat much meat normally, but when we went to visit people, especially my parents, there was a problem because they always cooked great big dinners with meat in them.

Unit 6, Lesson 3, Activity 3

Yes, I shared a room when I was at university. That was with someone called Phil. It wasn't very successful. Actually it's very difficult to share a room with someone. First of all, he was a bit untidy and I'm actually quite a tidy person. I like to be tidy. Secondly, he didn't like visitors, so when I invited friends round I felt that I was disturbing him quite a bit. We also got up at different times so, in the morning, he got up earlier than me and played the radio very loud, which annoyed me. I suppose the worst thing was I didn't really like him.

Unit 7, Lesson 1, Activity 1

Roy: Well, I left home when I was 20. I suppose the main reason why I left home was I wanted to be independent, know what I mean? You know, come home when I wanted and go out when I wanted and so on. So I left home and went to live in a flat.
David: Well, I finally left home because I had a lot of problems living with mum and dad – well, especially dad, we had a lot of problems. So when Roy decided to leave home and get a flat I said I'd share with him, so we got a flat together, him and me. And at that time, it was four years ago, I was 22 then. And we've been sharing ever since.

Unit 7, Lesson 2, Activity 2

Interviewer: Jacky, have you ever lived in another country?
Jacky: Yes, about fifteen years ago I lived in Sudan for two years.
Interviewer: What was it like?
Jacky: Well, it was very interesting, very different from England of course. But I found the main problem was I couldn't speak the language – they speak Arabic there – and I couldn't read it. I had a dictionary but I couldn't use that because I didn't even know the alphabet.

Unit 7, Lesson 2, Activity 3

Interviewer: And did not knowing the language cause you any problems when you got there?
Jacky: Yes and no. I found that when I was in a taxi I had to … to speak Arabic because the taxi drivers didn't speak any English at all. They didn't know where to go, so I had to say, 'Turn right, turn left, go straight on,' that kind of thing. But in restaurants they did speak English, that is the waiters spoke English, and there was no problem, that was very straightforward.
Interviewer: And how about shopping?
Jacky: Shopping in the market was hard. I had to speak Arabic, and I had to be able to read what was written on the price labels, and that was a different … the numbers were different.
Interviewer: And did you travel round much while you were there?
Jacky: Yes, we did. We travelled around in a jeep most of the time. That was alright but once we broke down, the jeep broke down when we were in a small village.
Interviewer: And did that cause problems then?
Jacky: No it didn't, funnily enough the mechanic could understand us. We spoke English and he spoke Arabic, but a lot of the words about cars and parts of cars are nearly the same, and he mended the jeep, no problem.

Unit 7, Lesson 3, Activity 4

Interviewer: Why did you leave home, Nigel?
Nigel: Well, four of us in one house was just too much.
Interviewer: And how did you do it?
Nigel: Andrea and I planned it very carefully. I gave up my London job and we moved out of our house and left it to the kids.
Interviewer: Hm … How are they managing without you?
Nigel: OK. They both have jobs and they pay their own bills. They rent out our old bedroom to a friend. I think it's doing them good.
Interviewer: And what about you and Andrea?
Nigel: We've found a new house in the country – just big enough for two of us – and I've got a new job in a bookshop. We're poorer, but happier!

Unit 8, Lesson 1, Activity 3

Sarah: Mike, do you think there will be problems with food for the world in the next hundred years?
Mike: Well, yes, I think we <u>will</u> probably all have problems with food for the world, because the number of people in the world is growing all the time.
Sarah: And number two. 'Do you think there will be big changes in the world's weather?'
Mike: Well, yes, there might be, because even now in the last few years you can see the weather is changing a lot all over the world. So I … I think it's possible, yes.
Sarah: And number three. 'Do you think people will go to live on other planets?'
Mike: No, I don't think that will happen in the next hundred years.
Sarah: Why not?
Mike: Oh … because they're too far away, too uncomfortable, and too dangerous.
Sarah: What about number four. 'Do you think there will be one government for the world?'
Mike: No, I don't think so, because people and countries are so different.
Sarah: And number five. 'Do you think there will be another world war?'
Mike: Well, you can't be sure about these things … I suppose there might be. Horrible idea, but possible.
Sarah: And the last one 'Do you think people will live for longer?'
Mike: Yes, I think they will, because medicine is getting better all the time.

Unit 8, Lesson 2, Activity 1

Reporter: Alison, what are you going to do when you leave school?
Alison: Well, next year I'm going to university, but first of all I want to see the world and so I'm going to go to Australia.
Reporter: Oh … why Australia? It's a long way, isn't it?
Alison: Yes, but I think it sounds great … you know, the life style, the beaches, and that.
Reporter: And er … what about the money for the plane ticket?
Alison: Well, I'm doing a Saturday job working in a pizza restaurant.
Reporter: And what are you going to do when you get there?
Alison: Well, I'll have to get a job because I want to stay for a long time – maybe nine months or so.
Reporter: And are you going on your own?
Alison: No, I'm going with a friend, Louise, she's a really good friend. So we'll try to get jobs in Australia working in bars or restaurants and save up some money, then go off and travel round the country. That's the plan anyway.
Reporter: Well, good luck … have a good time.
Alison: Thanks.

Unit 8, Lesson 3, Activity 3

I finished my journalism course last week. I thought I had a job starting next week, but they phoned and said I can't start until October, that's three months! I've fixed up a job in Italy. So it's a working holiday for me this year. It's lucky that my friend Pete phoned to tell me about the farm where he's working. They need more people to help so I'm going to go there and pick fruit. The farmer's agreed to give me a job for three months. I can get a student ticket for the train so it won't cost too much. It …'it won't be exactly relaxing, but at least it'll be sunny, and it won't break the bank.

Unit 8, Lesson 3, Activity 4

My aunt Susan's amazing!
She's 70 this year but she told me she's bored and she wants a change.
She's not going to stay at home any more.
She's not going to listen to the radio any more.
And she's not going to clean the house any more.
She's tired of all that, it's time for a change, so she's off!
She's going to get a plane to the sunshine.
She's going to stay in a five-star hotel.
She's going to spend all her money on cocktails and discos.
She's going to have the time of her life
This year!

Unit 9, Lesson 1, Activity 5

1 – Emma
I did a lot of revision for my exam at the end of school. When I looked at the exam paper I was really pleased because the first question was just what I wanted. I wrote and wrote, and I was still answering question one when the teacher said, 'You have five minutes left'. And I was only just finishing question one when she said, 'Stop writing now, please'. And there was question two and question three to do, and I didn't have any time left. And, of course, I failed the exam, even though I'm sure question one got a good mark!

2 – Annie
My brother, when he was taking an exam, he was only eleven, it was I think a six-page exam and he turned over two pages at the same time and so he missed two complete pages of questions … and failed the exam.

3 – Helen
I took my first French exam when I was about twelve, and I remember I did a lot of revision for it because I wanted to do well, and I revised all the words … all the new vocabulary. And then when I saw the exam the questions were all grammar, they didn't test vocabulary at all, and when I got the results I found I'd failed.

4 – Mike
In my first year at university I remember, um … I had a maths exam. It was on a Monday, so I decided to revise really hard all weekend in order to pass it.
Well, I was just starting work on the Saturday morning when the phone rang. The football team needed an extra player for a big match. So I didn't have time for any revision that day. Then I was just sitting down to do some work on the Sunday morning when the phone rang again. It was my grandmother's birthday and, er … there was a big family party. So finally I started to revise at 10.00 on Sunday evening and I worked all night.
But when I started the exam next morning, all the numbers were still going round and round in my head. So I, I walked out after half an hour and of course I failed the exam.

Unit 9, Lesson 1, Activity 6

In my first year at university I remember, um … I had a maths exam. It was on a Monday, so I decided to revise really hard all weekend in order to pass it.
Well, I was just starting work on the Saturday morning when the phone rang – the football team needed an extra player for a big match. So I didn't have time for any revision that day. Then I was just sitting down to do some work on the Sunday morning when the phone rang again. It was my grandmother's birthday and, er … there was a big family party. So finally I started to revise at ten o'clock on Sunday evening and I worked all night.
But when I started the exam next morning, all the numbers were still going round and round in my head. So I, I walked out after half an hour and of course I failed the exam.

Unit 9, Lesson 2, Activity 4

Victoria: Well, it was fun seeing dad go off to school but then I had to do the housework … it got a bit boring and I missed my friends.
Mr Evans: The worst thing was going into the classroom at first – I felt a bit stupid to tell you the truth. But they were really nice to me and the best thing was the history lesson. I really enjoyed that.

Unit 9, Lesson 3, Activities 2 and 3

Rachel: I went with a group of friends and they could all do it, so I wanted to learn too and the mountains are so beautiful with all the snow, and the feeling is so wonderful … It was very hard at the beginning, you're afraid of falling, and I think it's very important to learn from a professional … they teach you in easy stages and they build your confidence little by little. The most important thing is to learn how to stop!

Sheree: I felt that it was an important qualification needed for my job. I learnt at college. I did an evening course. First they gave us instructions, then we sat in front of the machine and did it. I use it a lot now in my job and I ask other people to help me if I have a problem – that's the best way to learn really.

Bruce: I don't know why I started, there's no reason really. I enjoy being up there in the sky, and I enjoyed very much learning about the technical side of it. I learnt about the technical side from books, but of course you have to have an instructor for the practical part, when you fly the plane. He sits next to you and you go up together, and if there's a problem he takes control.

Unit 10, Lesson 1, Activities 3 and 4

1 –

Alison: I'm sorry I couldn't come to your party but this is for you. Happy birthday!

Helen: Oh, a leather belt! Thank you … it's lovely. I really needed a belt to wear with my black trousers.

Alison: Ah!

2 –

Sarah: Hi! How are you feeling?

Paul: Oh, not too bad.

Sarah: I thought this might come in useful.

Paul: Oh, that's great. Thanks a lot. The food here's awful and I love cake. Is it chocolate? Mmm.

3 –

Man: Congratulations. This is for you and Mike.

Emma: Oh, I wonder what it is … oh, thank you very much. It's just what we wanted. Now I can read in bed. Look, Mike, a bedside lamp.

4 –

Woman 1: And this is something for the baby.

Jan: Isn't that sweet … he'll love that. Look, a lamb.

5 –

Woman 2: Congratulations! Here's something to help you celebrate!

John: Oh, thank you. They're just what we wanted. We'll have a drink in them tonight.

Unit 10, Lesson 2, Activity 2

Phil: Hello?

Helen: Hi, Phil, it's Helen.

Phil: Oh, hi Helen. How are you?

Helen: Fine thanks. Listen, Phil, I'm having a party. Would you like to come?

Phil: Yes, great. What's it for? Anything special?

Helen: Well, it's my 21st birthday.

Phil: I know that! So, when's the party?

Helen: A week on Saturday – that's the sixth of April. Can you come at about eight? You know where I live, don't you?

Phil: More or less. It's Hanger Lane isn't it? What's the number?

Helen: 119. Oh, and by the way, do you know Baz's address? I want to invite him and he's not on the phone.

Phil: Wait a minute and I'll find it. . er …, Baz Wilson isn't it, yes. Here he is, 117… College Road, … Leeds and the post code's LS17 … 2HN.

Helen: 117 … College Road, … Leeds … what was the post code?

Phil: LS17 2HN.

Helen: OK, thanks a lot. So I'll see you on the 6th.

Phil: Great! See you, Helen.

Helen: Bye.

Unit 10, Lesson 2, Activity 3

I'm really looking forward to the party. Most of my friends from school and college are coming and some of the neighbours too – there'll be about thirty people. We're having quite simple food – cheese, French bread, crisps, pizza, things like that. Maybe some salad as well. To drink – well, beer and wine, and soft drinks too, orange juice and stuff. The music's going to be great – we've hired a juke box for the party and you can choose the records – so we've got a real mixture – 60s and 70s music as well as new stuff, disco, rock 'n' roll, salsa, pop, a bit of everything. So I hope there'll be lots of dancing and everyone will enjoy themselves.

Unit 10, Lesson 3, Activity 3

Man 1: At the end of school, that was the final year at school, we all went to a club together, nearly everyone from our year – it was great!

Man 2: I did a German course in the evenings last year and at the end of the course we had a party at the teacher's house, it was really nice.

Woman 1: When I finished university we had a formal dance in the university hall, and all the girls wore long dresses and the men wore dinner jackets, and it was all very romantic.

Man 3: Last year I got a new job in a new town, so the night before I moved away I went out for a drink with my friends and flatmates.

Woman 2: On my last day at work I felt really sad but that evening I went out for a meal at a restaurant with all my friends and then we went to a disco and I didn't get home until five in the morning.